REFERENCE

H		Forts and Batteries
B		
C		
S V W X Y		Beaches where Brit
		Metalled Road
		Rough Waggon Trac
		Heights in Feet

Scale

GALLIPOLI

[The A

THE NAVY IN THE DARDANELLES
CAMPAIGN

THE NAVY IN THE DARDANELLES CAMPAIGN

ADMIRAL OF THE FLEET
LORD WESTER-WEMYSS, G.C.B.

The Naval & Military Press Ltd

Reproduced by kind permission of the Central Library,
Royal Military Academy, Sandhurst

Published by

The Naval & Military Press Ltd

Unit 10, Ridgewood Industrial Park,

Uckfield, East Sussex,

TN22 5QE England

Tel: +44 (0) 1825 749494

Fax: +44 (0) 1825 765701

www.naval-military-press.com

www.military-genealogy.com

© The Naval & Military Press Ltd 2010

The Naval & Military Press ...

...offer specialist books for the serious student of conflict. The range of titles stocked covers the whole spectrum of military history with titles on uniforms, battles, official histories, specialist works containing Medal Rolls and Casualties Lists, and numismatic titles for medal collectors and researchers.

The innovative approach they have to military bookselling and their commitment to publishing have made them Britain's leading independent military bookseller.

In reprinting in facsimile from the original, any imperfections are inevitably reproduced and the quality may fall short of modern type and cartographic standards.

INTRODUCTION

THE unsuccessful issue of the Dardanelles Campaign has tended to relegate it to a position of less importance in the history of the Great War than it deserves.

For ten months were the Allies battering at the outer gate of Constantinople in the well-grounded hope of bringing hostilities to an early conclusion, a hope destined to be shattered, not through the fault of the men on the spot but by the action of those in whose hands lay the conduct of the War. During those ten months British and French forces, both naval and military, were engaged in an amphibious warfare that called forth deeds of heroism and endurance second to none that history can show, and if the particulars of the expedition are not as well known as their merits entitle them to be it is largely because official reports and despatches can only, from their very nature, convey but an imperfect idea of such varied and ever varying incidents.

Some time must necessarily elapse before any complete and satisfactory history of this unique campaign can be given to the world, for it will only be after the publication of private letters and diaries that there can be produced any full narrative of the desperate struggle maintained with so much ardour and gallantry on both sides.

This volume has not the pretension of being a

history, it is a record of some of the events forming but a part of the whole and has been written in the hopes that it may help the historian of the future to clothe the dry bones of official documents with the cloak of reality. With this object I have published my letters without alteration, with their frequent repetitions and all their imperfections of style, believing that, written as they were in the very midst of the struggle, at odd moments when time admitted, they will convey a truer impression of the atmosphere in which we lived and had our being and a clearer idea of our hopes and views than anything written subsequently could possibly do.

It had been my original intention to relate only such events as came under my personal observation, making use of these letters and my diaries for the purpose, but I found that strict adherence to this plan could only result in a somewhat disconnected story losing much of its interest for the general reader from lack of continuity. I have therefore had recourse to other sources for information of incidents with which I was not myself connected and asked some of my comrades for an account of their personal experiences. In response Admiral Sir Cecil Thursby has kindly furnished me with the highly interesting description of the landing of the Australian and New Zealand forces at Gaba Tepe on April 25, reproduced in his own words in Chapter IV, while Admiral Grasset has been so good as to supply me with the details of the French operations at Kume Kale, of which Admiral Guépratte, too, has placed his recollections at my service.

To Captain Unwin, V.C., R.N., I am indebted for

much of the information concerning occurrences on board the *River Clyde* during those momentous hours that the troops were imprisoned in her. But what pen can describe the scenes on board that ship ? The memory of those crowded hours, fresh as they must ever be in the minds of those who lived through them, can never be adequately translated into words ; the story, however imperfectly told, will for all time remain enshrined amongst the heroic deeds that adorn the pages of history and form the proud heritage of our race.

And in an equal degree may this be said of the work of the submarines in the Sea of Marmora, whose crews for weeks on end uninterruptedly pursued their perilous operations never for one instant free from dangers of every description. Surely no work of fiction ever set forth deeds of greater daring and courage than those of which, owing to the kindness of Captain Nasmith, V.C., R.N., I have been able to give some account.

To all these officers I tender my grateful thanks for the assistance they have given me in my efforts to bring to the knowledge of the public some of those events which go far to prove that it is possible for failure to be as glorious as success.

This story was written before the second volume of Mr. Winston Churchill's work, *The World Crisis*, appeared, in which the same subject has been dealt with, but though it reveals much hitherto unknown to me it contains nothing that causes me to modify my views as set forth in Chapters XI and XII.

WESTER-WEMYSS.
A.F.

CHAPTER I

THE early days of February, 1915, found me flying my flag on board H.M.S. *Eclipse* (Captain Mitchell) in Plymouth Sound.

Since the outbreak of war I had been in command of a cruiser squadron perpetually patrolling the mouth of the Channel, a duty which, as time wore on, appeared to me of ever-decreasing utility, whilst the presence of enemy submarines in those waters since the month of October rendered it one of ever-increasing risk.

The Admiralty had evidently come to the same opinion, for on January 25 I received orders to limit the movements of my squadron to a more confined area, in order, as they told me, to diminish the chances of one of my ships being torpedoed. To my mind, however, the proposed alteration would only have had the opposite effect. For the purpose, therefore, of laying my views before their Lordships, together with a plan I had evolved for a patrol of trawlers, I took the first opportunity afforded by my flag-ship going into harbour to coal, to proceed to London.

The Staff accepted my views, but whatever the merits of my proposals for the trawler patrol may have been, they could not be put into execution on account of a want of vessels. On this occasion I gained an insight into the official mind, from the remark made to me : " We cannot have one of the four-funnellers (H.M.S. *Euryalus* and H.M.S. *Bacchante*, which were part of my squadron) sunk. The public would not stand it." A sentiment I shared, though not for the same reason, and did not confine to four-funnellers.

The ultimate result was that on February 2 I was ordered to take my squadron into Plymouth Sound and to await orders whilst the *Euryalus*, in which I had hitherto been flying my flag, and the *Bacchante* were withdrawn for service elsewhere.

There followed a wearying and exasperating time of lying idle, with nothing to do, but to await orders that never came, unable to give leave to either officers or men. I spent hours cursing my fate, for as far as I could see, there was but little hope of any change.

Suddenly, at 4 a.m., on Saturday, February 13, I received a telegram directing me to report myself at the Admiralty that afternoon. On my arrival I saw the First Lord (Mr. Winston Churchill), who informed me that it was proposed to send an expedition out to East Africa for the purpose of capturing the German cruiser *Königsberg*, which had taken refuge up the Rufigi River, the naval forces on the spot not being of sufficient strength for the purpose. I was to have command of this expedition and to be given a brigade of marines, besides a couple of cruisers. The *Königsberg* once captured or destroyed a new station on the East Coast of Africa was to be formed under my command.

My spirits rose to untold heights at the prospect of this welcome change from the monotony of the last six months and there followed a breathless forty-eight hours of trying to collect a kit suitable to the climate I thought myself bound for and information from the Admiralty, the former more easily obtainable than the latter. A flying visit to Plymouth to turn over the command of my dwindling squadron to the Senior Captain and I was back in London on the 16th lunching with friends in Chesham Place, preparatory to a final interview with the First Lord when, in the middle of the meal, I was called to the telephone and curtly informed by some unknown voice at the Admiralty that the expedition was off. My feelings can better be imagined than described. I went to Whitehall in a towering rage, for from the message I had gathered that it was my appointment which had been cancelled and not the expedition. After considerable delay I at length waylaid the First Lord in the corridor and accompanied him to his room, but before I could open my mouth he informed me that the project of dealing with the *Königsberg* was postponed, that it had that morning been decided to attempt to force the Dardanelles, and that the island of Lemnos, to be ceded to us by Greece, would be the base of operations. I was to be Governor of the island and to command the base, and he wished me to proceed there with the utmost despatch, adding that my orders would follow, which as a matter of fact they never did.

Whilst I was in the Naval Secretary's room after bidding good-bye to the First Lord, Lord Fisher came in. I had not spoken to him since the year 1908, when he had proposed to me to become Naval Secretary, at the same time adding that such an appointment would be a gross job since there were many men senior to me who ought to be preferred ;

plainly intimating that the price I should have to pay would be absolute subserviency to his views. I had indignantly refused to accept the post under such conditions, though it was the one I most coveted at the time, and from that time on there had been no sort of communication between us. When therefore he came towards me with outstretched hand the situation was not without its embarrassments, but—war was raging, he was First Sea Lord, I a Junior Rear Admiral, so I resolved to let bygones be bygones and whilst somewhat reluctantly taking the proffered hand, could not help remarking that the war brought odd people together. Beyond telling me that it was a big thing to which I was being sent, he gave me neither orders nor information, nor did he impart to me any indication as to the line of conduct he wished me to pursue. Thus I started off to assume my new duties without any instructions, and beyond an outline of the plans for bombarding the forts from Admiral Sir Henry Jackson, no enlightenment as to possible developments.

From patrolling the Channel to a cutting-out expedition in East Africa, from East Africa to the Dardanelles, such were the quick changes presented to me in the course of forty-eight hours, and the short interval between leaving the Admiralty late in the afternoon and my departure the next morning gave me but little time to make many necessary arrangements and to get together my staff. Captain Mitchell, who since war broke out commanded H.M.S. *Eclipse* in my squadron, came as flag-captain. Paymaster Miller, who had served as my secretary before, but who in August, 1914, had not been available, and Lieut.-Commander Bevan, my flag-lieutenant ever since I had hoisted my flag, accompanied me when I started from London at noon next day, February 17.

On our arrival in Paris on the following morning (it took thirteen hours to perform the journey from Boulogne), we found that there was no train leaving for Marseilles until the evening, so I had the whole day in which to visit friends and acquaintances. A call at the Ministry of Marine did not afford me any information and I could hear nothing of any French co-operation at the Dardanelles. Paris seemed as changed from the Paris I remembered a few months before as it was possible to be. I was much struck by the number of women in deep mourning to be seen in the streets, yet every one appeared calm and confident and with no doubts as to the ultimate result. Madame de B. told me that she could hardly believe that the France of that day was the same country as the France of six months before. Politics, she assured me, no longer existed, and now at last the right men were being allowed to come to the front.

The passage from Marseilles to Malta was made in the paquebot *Caledonian*, of whose comforts I have not very agreeable recollections, but it was a relief to find oneself at sea under conditions so different from those I had lately been accustomed to. The enemy submarines had not yet penetrated into the Mediterranean, there was therefore no necessity for the closed scuttles and want of illumination at night which rendered life at sea in Northern waters so stuffy and gloomy.

Malta was reached on the morning of the 22nd,

and an eight-hour stay there enabled me to have long conversations with Admiral Limpus, the Admiral Superintendent, who, up to the outbreak of war, had been Commander-in-Chief of the Turkish Navy. His view was that the forts of the Dardanelles once demolished, Turkey as a political unit would cease to exist. He described the Turkish population as loathing the Germans and bitterly opposed to the German Alliance, and believed that as soon as they felt the real pressure of war, they would refuse to fight any longer.

H.M.S. *Dartmouth* conveyed us to Mudros, where we arrived on the evening of the 24th, having previously anchored off Tenedos to enable me to visit Vice-Admiral Carden, commanding the squadron blockading the Straits which, I found, had commenced their bombardment of the outer forts on the 19th. Rear-Admiral de Robeck, with his flag flying in H.M.S. *Vengeance*, was Second in Command.

During my hurried interview with the First Lord he had briefly told me that an attack on the Dardanelles was impending, that the island of Lemnos was to be handed over to us, that I was to administer it as Governor and form a base at Mudros for the naval and military forces that were to take part in the operations, and he had informed me that instructions would follow. When, therefore, I visited Admiral Carden, I had hoped to obtain some more definite information and was proportionately disappointed that he had none to give me, beyond the fact that it was only the harbour and the town of Mudros, and not the whole island, that was to be in my hands. He gave me to understand that some 10,000 troops might shortly be expected, but of any plans for combined operations he appeared to be as ignorant as I was. There were already at Mudros a brigade of marines under the command of Colonel Trotman; they were embarked in the two transports *Braemar Castle* and *Cawdor Castle* in instant readiness to disembark and demolish the forts as they were silenced, and therefore could not be used by me for any other purpose. And so I entered into my kingdom with but vague ideas of what I had to prepare for, but always hopeful that I should shortly receive some further instructions, however indefinite they might be.

The splendid harbour of Mudros, capable of sheltering hundreds of vessels, was almost empty when I entered it; one of the battleships of the blockading squadron coaling, a couple of colliers for the Fleet, the two transports carrying the Marine Brigade, a supply ship, two or three destroyers and their parent-ship, the *Blenheim*, were all that greeted my eye. To the latter ship I transferred myself from the *Dartmouth*, much I fear to the disgust of her gallant Captain Coode, who naturally viewed with dismay the incursion of an Admiral and his staff into his already not too extensive accommodation. Personally I was delighted to find myself on board any ship, for I had feared having to take up my quarters in some house on shore.

I knew Lemnos well. Many a time had I visited the island when a lieutenant serving in H.M.S. *Undaunted* and H.M.S. *Astræa*, and later on when commanding H.M.S. *Suffolk*. I had tramped many a mile over its hills after partridge; I had joined in many a picnic on the shores of its harbour, but never had I realized the poverty of the country

2

or the entire lack of any of the ordinary adjuncts of civilization until the morning of February 25, when I landed to discover its resources. I wanted piers, cranes, water—there was nothing I did not want, and I found a complete absence of anything that could be of use to me.

Mudros is a little town boasting at that time of but one small crazy wooden pier for the convenience of fishing boats, a church, between sixty and eighty houses, some built of stone, others of mud and timber, a bad road leading to Kastro, the capital at the other side of the island, and nothing else. I found a Greek naval officer of the rank of Paymaster in charge of a small naval garrison, whose duties apparently consisted in preventing the guns and searchlights at the mouth of the harbour deteriorating from disuse. He was in some embarrassment as to his position towards me, and his attitude can best be expressed in his own words when he informed me that he was in no position to oppose any measures I might think fit to take. These words, uttered in the month of February in a somewhat cold and cynical tone, were repeated later on in a warm and friendly manner, and I am glad to say that in the course of time he proved a hearty and sympathetic co-operator.

The presence of this officer came as a complete surprise to me, for after what I had been told I did not anticipate to find any official—unless, indeed, the mayor—on the spot, and not knowing the attitude I was expected to assume, I was confronted by a situation pregnant with possible difficulties, all the greater as I was in total ignorance of the political state of affairs. This curtailment of the sphere of my authority was a very real drawback, rendering, as it did, a thousand times harder the task of ensuring the safety of the base. It was neither the enemy's fleet nor the enemy's forces against which precautions had to be taken. It was spies, secret agents, mischievous neutrals, babblers, and adventurers of all sorts that I had to guard against, and how this was to be achieved in a harbour the larger portion of whose shores were not under my jurisdiction, in a town whose inhabitants owed no allegiance to the English flag, with a Greek garrison at the capital only a few miles distant of whose dispositions I knew nothing, was a problem difficult of solution. There was but one bright spot—I had received no instructions; I would ask for none and would choose my own way to salvation or damnation.

There was a land telegraph line connecting Mudros with Kastro, where it joined up with the Eastern Telegraph Company's system. The not-over intelligent Greek clerk in charge informed me he was a Government official and could not guarantee either the early transmission or delivery of telegrams owing to the bad condition of the line. Giving him the choice of either becoming an official of the E.T.C. or of my commandeering the line and handing it over to that Company, while undertaking that the British Government should indemnify the Greek Government, I sent for the Manager of the E.T.C. at Kastro, bidding him put the line into working order. Fortunately at this juncture I was saved any further difficulties in the matter by the arrival of Mr. Cotterell, the Head Manager of the E.T.C. at Athens, whom the Admiralty sent to join my staff. He took the matter in hand and I never asked any inconvenient questions on the subject and was quite content to remain in ignorance of his *modus operandi* so long as he fulfilled my requirements, which he did in the highest degree.

Another welcome addition to my staff was Mr. Lukach, at that time a Civil Servant in the Government Service at Cyprus, who proved invaluable as " Government Secretary," a post improvised for the occasion. His intimate knowledge of Greeks and Turks, of their manners, customs and languages, eminently fitted him to deal with the administration of Mudros, and all through the ensuing ten months, when never a day passed without difficulties occurring the overcoming of which needed tact and firmness, did he carry out his peculiar and varying duties with success. To him I explained my views and wishes as regards the surveillance and treatment of the inhabitants, and since these included matters magisterial, municipal, financial and sanitary some idea may be gathered of the variety of subjects I had to deal with.

To guard as much as possible against the presence of spies it was necessary to obtain a knowledge of the inhabitants, and this could only be done with the help of the mayor, a local shop-keeper whose interests unfortunately ran counter to mine. I had to try and enlist his sympathies and good will, but it was expecting too much to suppose that he would cordially adopt my point of view and carry out wishes that would naturally cause both him and his fellow-townsmen considerable inconvenience. So, in spite of his assurances of assistance, I knew that I should never get satisfactory results until I had some means of enforcing my orders. These did not come to my hand until the arrival of a battalion of Australian troops, who were disembarked and encamped close to the village on March 7. Even then I could never rely upon their services, for their commanding officer required them constantly for drills and route marches. Their presence alone, however, had a beneficial moral effect.

These episodes merely exemplify the endless difficulties to be contended with and were solely due to the anomalous position I had been placed in. Appointed in London Governor of an island which on my arrival I found being governed by its own legitimate officials, administering a town over whose inhabitants I had no legal authority, commanding a base situated in a territory that was in theory if not in fact neutral and for whose safety and well-being I was responsible, my task was rendered none the easier from my entire ignorance of the actual political situation. Was Greece a secret ally ? or was she a neutral, whose neutrality was being flagrantly violated ? What was her position towards the Entente Powers or theirs towards her ? It was only in the light of knowledge gained much later that I began to understand her attitude towards the Allies during the Gallipoli campaign.

The ideal of a great Greek Empire, with Constantinople as its capital, had for generations been the dream of the Greeks, many of whom regarded the marriage of the Crown Prince Constantine with the Princess Sophia of Germany as part fulfilment of the ancient prophecy that sovereigns of these names should be the first to reign over this re-born Empire. The Balkan wars of the last years had pointed to the coming end of Turkish domination and the

outbreak of the European conflagration in 1914
appeared likely to hasten it. In the success of the
Entente Powers Greece saw a possible realization
of her ambitions ; it cannot therefore be doubted
that it was not purely altruistic motives that led
her to make an offer of assistance to the Allies in
August, 1914, but the hopes of reaping a tangible
reward. When, however, in March, 1915, it began
to be known that the possession of Constantinople
had been promised to Russia, when moreover the
Russian Government stipulated that no Greek
troops were to be allowed to enter in or within a
given radius of Constantinople, the situation underwent a radical change. It could hardly be expected
that Greece would throw in her lot with those whose
victory would put an end once and for all to her
ambitions, and no Government, no statesman, would
have been sufficiently powerful to induce the country
to plunge into a war on the side of the combatants
whose declared aims were in direct contradiction
to its national interests. The fall of M. Venizelos
in March, 1915, was not, as has so often been
asserted, the cause of the estrangement of Greece
from the Allies, but rather was this estrangement the
cause of his fall. The promise of Constantinople
to Russia had the logical and inevitable result of
converting Greece from a potential ally into a covert
opponent, for her interests now lay in the opposite
camp and her position in consequence became one
of extraordinary difficulty. Deeply committed to
the Allies by her early proffer of assistance, it was
no longer in her aims to further an expedition whose
success would shatter her most cherished hopes.
On the other hand, her geographical situation, her

exposed coast and defenceless harbours placed her at the mercy of those Powers in whose hands rested the command of the sea. Between the two contending parties Greece, therefore, was obliged to steer a prudent if somewhat ambiguous course, and wrapping herself in the remaining shreds of her tattered neutrality, adopted henceforth a line of passive resistance to both sides, from which neither threats nor promises, neither bullyings nor cajoleries, nor the most intensive propaganda was able to move her.

CHAPTER II

IF Lemnos was unable to provide all that I wanted, Malta Dockyard could and did supply many of the deficiencies. Admiral Limpus responded to my demands in a manner I must ever be grateful for.

My chief source of anxiety lay in the shortness of fresh water. I had from the very beginning ascertained that the local supply was only just sufficient for the wants of the inhabitants, and I knew that I should very shortly be called upon to satisfy the needs of some thousands of men. I telegraphed to the Admiralty asking for condensing ships, only to receive the reply that none were available and that I must make use of the water the island contained, " which," the telegram added, " the *Mediterranean Pilot* (an unofficial publication, a sort of Mariners' Guide to the Mediterranean) informed them was plentiful."

It is true that it would not have been impossible to bring water down from the hills, and I had already sent an officer of the R.E., a detachment of which had arrived in the first transport, with a view to ascertaining what could be done in this way, but such an undertaking would have required too much time and labour and neither were at my disposition —for labour I had none and the troops were expected immediately. But Malta came to the rescue as ever and sent fresh water in the double bottoms of every ship that was despatched to Mudros—a slow and laborious method of providing it, but better than nothing.

On March 1 General Birdwood, commanding the Australian and New Zealand troops, arrived from Egypt in H.M.S. *Dublin* and it was from him that I learned for the first time that the number of troops that might be expected was nearer 40,000 than 10,000. He told me that so far no decision as to their employment had been reached, that this decision would probably rest upon the result of the naval bombardment of the forts which the bad weather had prevented from being consistently carried out since the commencement of the attack on February 19.

We landed together and looked for camping grounds. There were many suitable sites, but the shortage of water rendered it impossible to disembark more than a very limited number of men.

The following day, March 2, I took the General over to Tenedos to see Admiral Carden. The weather was still bad, but a bombardment was going on. We had a conference with the Admiral; he was evidently coming to the conclusion that the enemy's concealed guns and mobile batteries were rendering mine-sweeping impossible, and that they would have to be cleared away before any real progress could be made with the work of attacking the inner forts. To accomplish this troops would have to be landed upon the Peninsula and the question arose with how much opposition would such a landing meet? These matters would have to be settled elsewhere than at Mudros or Tenedos, but whatever the decision might be, it became increasingly clear to me that however many steamboats, tugs, lighters, etc., I might be able to procure from the Piræus or elsewhere, I should never have too many.

I suggested to the Admiral that a naval officer of some standing should accompany the General back to Egypt to enable us to keep closely in touch with the military authorities, and that the G.H.Q. should receive naval assistance in developing their plans. He did not, however, fall in with my idea, and indeed it was difficult for him to spare a suitable man, but so convinced was I of the necessity of this step that I detached Captain Mitchell, my flag-captain, for this purpose, much as I was in need of his services myself. Captain Mitchell never rejoined me and remained attached to the Army for the whole of the campaign.

General Birdwood returned to Egypt, and for the first time I began to have some conception of what might be required of the base.

On March 4 the vanguard of what eventually proved to be a large army arrived in the form of 5,000 Australians. Of these, 1,000 were landed and encamped close to the town, the others remaining afloat in their transports, principally on account of the lack of water.

The same day, the weather having cleared, the bombardment was continued. The *Braemar Castle* and the *Cawdor Castle* were sent out to Tenedos and the marines landed for the purpose of demolishing the forts silenced by the guns of the Fleet. They suffered, however, a severe check and had to be re-embarked without having been able to accomplish their task. For the next few days the operations were continued with an intensive fire, but on the 8th the attack was discontinued, for it was realized that no further progress could be made without considerable military assistance.

On the 9th a French General arrived who informed me that he had been told that I would supply the French troops shortly arriving with all that they required, a statement which in the possibilities that it implied gave me a severe shock. Their demands, however, did not turn out to be of any magnitude, and after marking out the areas for their encampments I was not called upon for any further help.

"March 9, 1915. . . . Imagine my feelings when this morning there appears on the scene a French General who informs me that he is the precursor of a French Army and has apparently been told that *I* will supply him with all that they need. Truly the ways of those in authority are beyond conception. This wretched island is evidently supposed to be a land flowing with milk and honey *and* water. But I am now in the mood that this rather amuses me, for I have no doubt that I shall manage. Fisher said that it was a big thing they were sending me to—I think he little imagined *how* big . . . it would be all plain sailing had I a proper staff and appliances, the latter are being scratched up anyhow in the best way that one can manage. . . . Everything seems very much at sixes and sevens at home so far as we are concerned. However I think I am getting the situation well in hand. . . . I have established a sort of Court Room on shore where I dispense justice, that is to say I hear claims for damages, etc. The inhabitants find circulating amongst them more money than they ever supposed existed in the whole world, and I need hardly say that they are perfectly delighted. The Australians

are the most magnificent body of men I have ever
seen. I thought the Canadians very fine as raw
material, but these men are even finer. One really
feels proud of one's Race. They are wild, of course,
but such pleasant-looking devils. I often go to their
camp and look round, and they always seem pleased
to see one. . . ."

On the 12th the *Franconia*, the first of the transports carrying the Royal Naval Division, some
8,500 strong, arrived. Major-General Paris, R.M.A.,
who commanded them, was on board with his staff.
He told me that his troops had been embarked in
such a manner that it was sufficient for a man to
be in one transport to be certain that his greatcoat
was in another; his whole force would have to be
disembarked, re-organized and re-embarked again
before they would be ready for service. He was
under the impression that this could be done at
Mudros, as apparently were the authorities at home ;
but it only needed a few words of explanation from
me to convince him of the absolute impossibility of
such a proceeding. We had neither wharves, nor
cranes, nor even landing piers and an insufficiency
of boats, and the only course to take was to send
the whole force to Egypt, where, at Alexandria or
Port Said, this complicated work could be carried
out. On my informing the Admiralty of this they
demurred to my proposal and wished the re-organization to take place at Mudros, but as I pointed out
it was not a matter of want of ability or good will
of anybody concerned but one of sheer impossibility
owing to the lack of appliances. And so this fleet
of transports, supposed to be in a state of readiness
for disembarking their cargoes, human and material,

on the scene of operations, had to turn back and be re-organized and re-stowed elsewhere.

These occurrences opened my eyes to the manner the preparations for this campaign were being undertaken, and never from that moment did I allow myself to entertain expectations that I felt would never be fulfilled. I realized that I must be prepared to organize everything on the spot and not rely upon the assistance of the authorities at home.

In the meantime the work of organizing the base and of collecting materials for what now seemed certain to prove a big combined naval and military operation was proceeding as fast as a lack of means and shortness of personnel would allow. A certain Mr. Vincent Grech, a Maltese, had been commissioned by the Admiralty to buy boats, lighters, etc., in the Mediterranean. I had not been able to get into touch with this gentleman since my arrival, and fortunately had employed agents of my own to purchase such craft. I say fortunately, because when Mr. Grech eventually turned up on March 26, it was only to tell me that an embargo had been laid on such purchases as he had made by the Governments of the various countries in which he had been acting. At the Piræus my agents had bought up all the suitable craft that they could lay their hands on, and these began to arrive in batches, but I experienced considerable difficulty in looking after them, for there were no bluejackets available and the Greeks whom I had to hire proved unreliable and unsatisfactory.

The gathering together of this great force acted as a magnet for all the dregs of the heterogeneous population of the Levant. It was indispensable that I should have the control of the traffic into Mudros both by sea and by land. The former was not difficult, and with three old torpedo boats sent from Malta an examination service was formed to deal with incoming vessels and a system of licensing boats and small ships trading with the other islands was instituted. This created a certain amount of dissatisfaction at first, but was eventually accepted by the seafaring population and continued to give good results during our occupation of the place. The control of the land traffic, however, was a much more difficult and complicated matter. With the assistance of such troops, British and French, as I could from time to time borrow for the purpose I formed a cordon, a very uncertain one it is true, which placed the eastern part of the island nominally under my control. But the western shore of the harbour with its uninterrupted communication with Kastro and the remainder of the island was a perpetual source of anxiety, for successful as I might be in keeping spies and undesirables by a system of passes out of the town of Mudros itself I had absolutely no control over the other side of the harbour.

About a fortnight after my arrival the officer commanding the Greek garrison at Kastro, in company with the Bishop of Lemnos, paid me an official visit. Now I felt that the success of my administration would depend very considerably upon the terms I might find myself on with these gentlemen. So after many complimentary speeches on both sides, which we all three recognized as meaning nothing at all, I produced some big cigars and large glasses of brandy that I had luckily been able to

obtain at Malta, and with this help managed to
persuade them to follow the line of conduct adopted
by their naval confrère at Mudros. Before they
left the ship they assured me that not only would
they put no difficulties in my way, but would even
render me assistance in any steps I should deem
necessary to take, so long, be it understood, that
they themselves were not called upon to intervene.
This attitude on their part encouraged me to per-
severe in the measures I was putting into force for
the suppression of espionage and for the well-being
of the troops, and after an extra big glass of brandy
and an extra large cigar I managed to wheedle out
of the Commandant permission to take care of the
guns at the mouth of the harbour, a care, I may add,
I had already exercised without his permission.
But in spite of the friendliness engendered presumably by the mellowness of the brandy there remained
a certain constraint on the part of both these officials baffling all my efforts to ascertain from them
whether their complaisance was on account of,
or in spite of, orders received from their Government.

The first practical result of this interview was
a system of passes without which no one was supposed to be able to pass the cordon or to leave or
enter the town; a system the Commandant certainly helped to carry out, whether to the best of
his ability or not I am unable to say, but certainly
not to my satisfaction.

At the end of March a different attitude on the
part of the Greek officials began to manifest itself.
Passes were issued more indiscriminately, and I
have every reason to believe that on one occasion at

least, a pass was actually wittingly issued to an
enemy spy.

Owing to this change of attitude I advised the
Admiralty that the only road to successful surveillance of the harbour lay in taking over the administration of the whole island, which with a very small
garrison could easily and readily have been accomplished. But I received no answer and had to
continue my efforts with the rather desponding feeling
that under such circumstances the safety of the
camps and depôts, now growing up on the shores
of the harbour, and of the transports and store-
ships lying at anchor therein could never be guaranteed. I was perfectly prepared to accept the
responsibility of certain measures without consulting the authorities in London, but the only
other step, the administration of martial law over
part of an island belonging to a neutral Power,
was one I naturally could not adopt on my own
authority.

" March 13, 1915. . . . My work seems to be as
all-embracing as it is perpetual. From allocating
land, adjusting compensation for damages, supplying
water, urging lazy people to do some work, landing armies, and organizing defences down to the
ordinary squadron work, nothing seems to pass me
by. Telegrams pouring in in basketsful, messages
by wireless telegraphy, orders from England (generally contradictory), requests from all parts of the
Mediterranean, demands for the possible and impossible from every quarter, this will give you some
idea of what I have to deal with at all hours of the
day and night. Merchant captains and military
officers seem to vie with each other in seeing which

can be the most tiresome, and all the time I know that one small exhibition of temper on my part at the wrong moment may do infinite harm. So you can imagine that I sometimes have a trying time. However it is all interesting and often amusing, and I am consoled by the presence of a delightful old Colonel of Engineers, who not only works well and quickly but sympathizes with me and is as full of humour and spirits as a boy of eighteen. He has been of great assistance to me, and between us we get through a marvellous amount of work in the twenty-four hours. The weather on the whole has not been unkind, and although the temperature is variable the sun is generally shining and the sunsets and lights are beautiful though the island itself is ordinary and uninteresting. You would have laughed had you been able to see me to-day settling the differences between a voluble and excited French Colonel and a stolid and obstinate English Major, both of whom wanted to pitch some tents on the same piece of ground, and neither of whom spoke or understood a word of anything except his own mother-tongue. Truly I felt that a Solomon would have been better fitted to deal with them than I, for each one of them was as much in the right as the other, inasmuch as neither had any claims at all, and both had to be satisfied. Luckily their ignorance of each other's language enabled me to say what I liked to either without being understood by the other, so in a few minutes I had them both settled on quite new territory, each one thinking that I had adjusted the dispute in his favour and what a 'damned good fellow' I was on one side and 'aimable camarade' on the other. . . . I flatter myself I have the mayor of Mudros in my pocket. This functionary appears to be the only banker, the only shop-keeper, the only publican and general Pooh-Bah of the place. Being a Greek I need hardly add that he is a Shylock and probably owns every inhabitant of the place body and soul. So far he seems to be acting on the square with me, and I think that the hopes of an eventual piece of ribbon, to say nothing of the money he must be amassing, will keep him bound to me during our occupation. . . ."

" March 14, 1915. . . . The work in the Dardanelles continues. There was some fighting last night, but I have not as yet received any particulars. Clearing the mine fields is the business in hand. The men are splendid. Volunteers were called for the other day for a particularly nasty and dangerous job, and every man volunteered. Certainly there is no lack of self-sacrifice on the part of the rank and file. One can only admire them and wish to God that all this loss of life were not necessary. . . ."

It was for mine-sweeping that volunteers were called, and this was necessitated by the failure of the crews of the mine-sweeping trawlers to face the heavy shell-fire they met with on their difficult and perilous task. They were splendid men who had proved their courage on many an occasion, but lacking in that discipline which alone enables a body of men to stand shell-fire.

The new volunteer crews carried through their task on the night of the 13th and succeeded in destroying many mines, though not the whole field, but the heavy casualties they suffered made it quite evident that the defence was stronger than the attack. Under these circumstances the method of overcoming the mines had to be changed. The only alternative lay in sweeping by daylight under the cover of intensive fire from battleships. This entailed a very heavy expenditure of ammunition that could ill be afforded, but since it was the only way the Navy could now succeed in pushing through the Straits without the assistance of the Army, a result so ardently desired by the Government, it was decided that the attempt should be made.

In the meantime ships and troops had fast been accumulating at Mudros. The first detachment of the French army had arrived on the 11th and the remainder were expected to be all assembled by the 17th. The Australian force also were all present. I was still chafing at the ignorance I was being kept in, never realizing that the plan of campaign, the knowledge of which I believed would be of such assistance to me, did not exist. It seemed so evident that whatever the result of the present operations might be Mudros must for a long time to come continue to be the base, that the failure of the military authorities to accede to my demands for building piers and erecting hospitals was inexplicable. They, however, did not share my opinion and believed that with a force, whatever its size, once landed upon the Peninsula, they would be able to push on to such an extent as to form a base close in their rear.

With the increasing number of ships and men the work of my all too small staff grew to such an extent that to cope with it became a matter of considerable difficulty. Commander Unwin, destined shortly

to cover himself with undying glory, and Commander
Escombe had now joined me, and their energy,
ability and cheerfulness helped us to overcome our
difficulties. We were all living on board the *Hussar*
and the *Imogene* for convenience sake moored alongside of each other. The former was an old gunboat
that had been converted into a yacht for the Commander-in-Chief of the Mediterranean, the latter
before the War had been the stationnaire at Constantinople. We were very cramped and no arrangement for our accommodation or for carrying out
our duties could well have been worse, but there was
no alternative. The weather too had been bad,
constant gales of wind making communication
difficult, and all these disadvantages did not tend
towards forwarding the proceedings. The Admiralty
had sent out a net-defence to be laid at the mouth
of the harbour and this was being carried out by
Lieutenant Munro, R.N.R., an officer of great experience, but a lack of men caused the progress to be
but slow. Enemy submarines however had not yet
penetrated so far afield, and as it turned out the
defence was finished before they eventually made
their appearance.

"March 15, 1915. . . . What tiresome people
soldiers can be! Everybody above the rank of
subaltern seems to think that he ought to have an
Admiral's barge at his own disposal. Of course
these stories only reach me through my staff and
they, poor devils, are worried to death by the help-
lessness of them all. Truly a soldier is not the man
of whom one can expect the manufacture of bricks
without straw. Ian Hamilton is expected here in
a couple of days, perhaps then I may hear of some

definite plan. So far I am quite in the dark as to what is proposed, and that does not make my work any the easier. . . ."

On March 16, in response to a message of the Vice-Admiral lying off Tenedos, I proceeded there in a destroyer and found him ill and obliged to give up the command. The situation thus created was a delicate one, for his departure would leave me the senior officer, since Rear-Admiral de Robeck, his second in command of the squadron operating against the forts, though older and senior to me in the Service, was actually my junior on the Rear-Admiral List. Here was I, organizing the base, an arduous task inevitably bound to suffer from a change of command, whilst de Robeck was in the middle of a complicated operation, in full possession of and knowing its most intricate details of which I was completely ignorant; yet surely the senior officer's place was with the squadron at the front. I discussed the situation from every point of view with him and with Commodore Keyes, his Chief of the Staff, and eventually made up my mind that no other course was open to me except to return to Mudros to carry on my work there, leaving the operations in de Robeck's hands. I accordingly telegraphed my decision to the Admiralty and added that if they considered it desirable to make de Robeck an acting Vice-Admiral, a step in my opinion very desirable on account of the presence of the French Rear-Admiral rendering the question of command otherwise difficult, I was ready to serve under de Robeck's orders. It is hardly necessary to state that I did not come to this conclusion without considerable heart-burning and a bitter feeling of disappointment, but I had no doubt in my mind that under the peculiar circumstances the decision was the right one to take and it had the happy result that for the remainder of the campaign de Robeck and I worked together with the greatest cordiality and friendship. And so I returned to Mudros, sore and disappointed I must confess, yet conscious of the correctness of my conduct.

The next day, the 17th, saw me once more at Tenedos, whither I went to attend a Council of War. Sir Ian Hamilton arrived there in the *Phæton* at the same time as I did in the *Dartmouth*, and the afternoon was spent on board the *Queen Elizabeth*, in which de Robeck, now a Vice-Admiral and my senior officer, had hoisted his flag. As a result of the conference it was decided that another attack on the forts was to be made the next day to cover a further attempt to sweep the mine field, and that on its upshot would depend the decision as to the extent and manner of the employment of the Army of which Ian Hamilton was to be Commander-in-Chief.

I returned to Mudros with a clearer conception of the military ideas than I had yet been able to get. General d'Amade, who had arrived to take command of the French troops, accompanied me.

D'Amade was a splendid specimen of a French officer who had won his laurels and the *médaille militaire* in N. Africa. We became fast friends and he often spoke openly to me. He told me that he was against landing on the Peninsula at all. He would have liked to leave Gallipoli severely alone and land the Army at Adramyti Bay and from thence march straight on to Constantinople and seize the inner key of the Dardanelles. This he considered would be the best way of helping the Navy to get through the Straits. The Constantinople-Smyrna Railway would in such a case have to be captured and seized at the point nearest to the landing-place and I went so far as to promise him to send a reconnoitring party to survey the Bay and the country between it and the railway. I actually procured a large fishing boat and organized a small party who, disguised as Greek fishermen, were to carry this out. These projects, however, came to nothing, for all operations in Asia Minor were banned by orders from England.

On the 18th was fought the naval battle resulting in the loss of the *Irresistible*, the *Ocean*, and the *Bouvet*, and very nearly in that of the *Inflexible*, only saved by the fine seamanship of her Captain (Phillimore) and the good work of all her officers and men ; a battle which finally put an end to all hopes of forcing the Dardanelles without the assistance of the Army. On the following day (the 19th) I again visited de Robeck at Tenedos and found him naturally enough somewhat depressed at the turn of events. He spoke of disaster, a term I begged him not to use, and after conferring with him on the steps necessary to take as a consequence of the battle of the day before I left him more cheerful than I had found him.

The experience we had undergone pointed to the following argument : the battleships could not force the Straits until the mine field had been cleared —the mine field could not be cleared until the concealed guns which defended them were destroyed— they could not be destroyed until the Peninsula was in our hands, hence we should have to seize it with the Army. Any main operations must therefore be postponed until such time as preparations for a combined attack could be made.

The surviving officers and men of the *Irresistible* and *Ocean* were now available and helped considerably towards pushing forward the work at Mudros. They were berthed on board the *Fauvette*, the ship the net-defence had been sent out in. She was small and unsuitable but better than nothing. Captain Dent became principal transport officer, Captain Hayes-Sadler of the *Ocean* assisted on shore, and the two navigating officers, now harbour masters, were entrusted with the arrangement for berthing, a most necessary charge since the large number of ships of all kinds perpetually coming in and out of the harbour began to test even its large capacity.

It had been blowing very hard ever since the 19th. On the 21st Torpedo Boat 064 on her way from Port Said to Mudros went ashore outside the harbour and became a total wreck, without happily any loss of life. Much damage, too, was caused to the lighters, of which some sank at their moorings, and though the greater portion were recovered a few of them had to be left at the bottom of the sea through lack of time and men to raise them.

General Birdwood returned from Egypt on the 21st in H.M.S. *Diana*, bringing with him Captain Mitchell, from whom I was able to gain much knowledge as to the military appreciation of the situation, and before he returned to Egypt in a few days' time to continue his work with the G.H.Q. I was in a position to give him instructions for his guidance.

At a meeting of Admirals and Generals held on

board the *Queen Elizabeth* in Mudros harbour on the 22nd the whole situation was reviewed, and the pros and cons for an immediate attempt at landing troops on the Peninsula were debated. Of the desirability for instant action there was never a doubt, but the chance of surprise—to my mind an absolute necessity for the success of such an enterprise—had vanished. The enemy was thoroughly on his guard and to throw the troops immediately available on shore in face of an almost certain stubborn defence without carefully prepared plans and with the transports unorganized was out of the question. Moreover these troops, though of splendid material, were not of the first line with the exception of the 29th Division which had not yet reached the scene.

The decision of the conference confirmed the conclusion de Robeck and I had come to on the 19th, viz. that combined action must be postponed until plans had been developed and perfected. In the meantime the Vice-Admiral would keep the enemy busy with constant bombardments. The breathing space thus afforded would also give time for a thorough re-organization of the mine-sweeping service, a matter entrusted to Captain Haneage of the *Albion*.

And so the meeting came to an end with perfect accord between the Navy and Army, and we each went our way to our several tasks, mine being, in addition to the command of the base, the preparation of the naval part of the combined operation.

" March 18, 1915. . . . it is a curious sight on shore. English and French camps pitched side by side and the difference between them very apparent. The former more elaborate and to the eye more methodical than the latter. The French bakeries are extremely elaborate and look almost like a street in Paris, but to my astonishment, and equally to theirs, their bread is not so good as ours which is baked in ordinary field ovens. The landing place is a curious medley, French uniforms of every description mingling with our khaki and with the peasants' and local fishermen's not unpicturesque clothes. The differences in national character come out very strongly when brought so close together in such a small space ; but all have one thing in common, a good-tempered gaiety which is pleasant to see. Mingling among them all is the wily Greek, avaricious and plausible, making much money out of both the others, hawking every sort of commodity from onions to Turkish Delight and Beecham's pills. Through all this motley crowd there is a continual stream of perspiring Australians carrying huge loads of stores and pushing improvised carts. They are magnificent specimens of the raw material of humanity. I think I have never seen finer. The natives are in the seventh heaven of delight, money pouring into their pockets. We are getting very full up now ; transports, supply ships, colliers of both nationalities fill the harbour and with each fresh arrival the work increases. . . ."

" . . . March 22, 1915. . . . I have had the very deuce of a time these last few days. Gales of wind that have done much damage. The transports are so helpless and their captains equally so under such circumstances—their boats get adrift, etc. A torpedo boat has gone ashore and become a total wreck but everybody saved. Some of the lighters that I bought at Athens are adrift somewhere, though I am in hopes that they may be recovered. . . . What I hate is all the amateurs that spring up on all sides. . . . Yesterday the French wanted to haul two Italians out of a Greek steamer because they suspected them, probably rightly, of being newspaper correspondents. Imagine the complications which might have arisen. Luckily I was in time to intervene.

" . . . March 24, 1915. . . . Still suffering from gales of wind which retard the work dreadfully. It makes boating and communication so slow, and goodness knows the means at our disposal are scanty enough without being retarded by bad weather. . . .

" . . . March 25, 1915. . . . Truly mine is a boisterous kingdom, so far as the weather is concerned I should say, for the inhabitants seem peaceful and law-abiding enough. But the weather! An incessant gale for a week now and it has done much damage. Several of my cherished lighters have been sunk and some of the tugs bought at the Piræus have not turned up. The confusion that has been caused by the slipshod manner in which the troops have been sent from England is something awful. The ships packed anyhow, things that belong to one battalion stowed at the bottom of the hold of a ship carrying another and so on all through. I cannot imagine what they have been thinking about. The same old story, I suppose, nobody knowing what anybody else is thinking of and at the head of affairs men ignorant of all technique who think they only have to say ' do this ' and it is done. And so the thing *is* done but in such a manner that it had much better be left undone.

And all this for an expedition the success of which absolutely depends upon accuracy of detail. Well —we shall no doubt put matters straight, but it requires time and patience. The Army, and indeed the Navy too, is swarming with strange people who are supposed to know all about Constantinople but whose services I cannot think can be of any real use. I am perpetually getting the offer of the services of such men to serve on my staff; my answers so far have invariably been the same. Yesterday I attended the funeral of a French officer who had died on board one of the French ships. It was a fine ceremony. The General, my friend d'Amade, made an excellent peroration at the grave-side, dignified, simple and full of eloquence. . . . How my heart goes out to the ancient Israelites who had to make bricks without straw! If you could imagine what the fatuous authorities seem to expect out of us here! They apparently think that because we have the use of the harbour from the Greeks and that I am here with the title of Governor and Senior Officer that they have established a base. Good God! I have *nothing*. But we struggle along and truly I am surprised at the results we obtain and lost in admiration at the resources of my people. I have connected my ship with the shore by telegraph cable and have transferred the censor's office to it. Under such circumstances the censorship is comparatively easy, the only thing that is, I have got the various newspaper correspondents well in hand and so far they have been most reasonable and easy to deal with." . . .

I remained to continue as ignorant as ever of the real state of the political situation and in conse-

quence listened greedily to all the stories emanating
from the Intelligence Department (for at that time
I had none of my own) and other sources. Rumours
were current about a *rapprochement* between Greece
and Bulgaria and I began to hope that our diplomacy might succeed in inducing these two countries
into war on the side of the Allies.

March 25 was Greek Independence Day and it
was freely said that public sentiment at Athens
might force the King to declare war against his will.
How far we were from the truth and how eager to
believe what would have so cleared the situation
for all of us !

The now universally known fact that a large
force was assembling at Mudros caused a fresh
recrudescence on the part of spies, unauthorized
newspaper correspondents, undesirables and adventurers of all sorts to attempt an entrance into the
place. Many were those turned back and many
the complaints received of people being refused
admittance who should have been allowed to enter.
Though no doubt there were some hard cases it is
certain that many got through the imperfect cordon
who should not, but my means of controlling this
traffic were so inadequate that I never had any
illusions on the subject.

It was at this juncture that Mr. Vincent Grech,
the before mentioned Admiralty Agent, arrived on
the scene. He was empty handed and tried with
much bounce and swagger to slur over his failure
to procure the needed craft. Having myself experienced but little difficulty on the part of my own
agents I lost all belief in him, and when he casually
observed that he had brought with him a naval

officer whom he grandiloquently described as his
A.D.C. I sent for the latter and was astounded to
recognize an old friend, whom for a long time I had
lost sight of, Commander H. V. Simpson, retired
from the Service many years before. He had an
extraordinary story to relate. He had no passport,
no papers of any kind and had been told to accompany Mr. Grech in order to keep an eye on his doings.
He had demurred at the false position he was thus
placed in, but he had been assured at the Admiralty
that he was carrying out a mission of the utmost
importance and would reap his reward in the future,
etc., etc. I had neither time nor inclination to
investigate the curious tale, but cut the matter short
by telling Mr. Grech I had no further use for his
services and giving Commander Simpson an appointment as transport officer where he did most excellent
work.

Though a goodly number of small craft were
gradually collected together considerable difficulty
was experienced in providing them with crews.
Many were manned by Greeks, who all protested
their willingness to see the matter through, but
though I attached little reliance to these professions,
I did hope that if the worst came to the worst, and
it should prove impossible to replace them by bluejackets before the expedition started, some at least,
attracted by the offer of good pay, would not play
me false so long as they were assured of not being
brought under fire.

In connection with this there occurred a somewhat ridiculous incident. •

A few days before we left Mudros one of the
tugs whose Greek crew had not yet been relieved,

broke down and the engineer officer sent to examine the engines reported the damage as wilful sabotage. The crew had adopted this means of ensuring their remaining in harbour and still, as they hoped, drawing the pay, and I feared that this example unless immediately and severely dealt with might prove contagious. With the object, therefore, of thoroughly frightening the delinquents, I stage-managed a little scene; the master and engineer of the boat playing the part of prisoners, the engineer officer that of witness, and I of judge and jury. To render it more dramatic so as to impress the so-called prisoners (over whom of course I had no legal authority whatever) I caused the inquiry to be held late in the evening when all the electric lights were out and dim lanterns gave the only illumination. After a searching cross-examination proving quite clearly that sabotage *had* been committed I addressed the men in my gravest manner, and after pointing out to them the heinousness of their offence and treachery of their conduct, sentenced them to be shot at dawn. I had never doubted but that this sentence would be received with dismay and appeals for mercy, but the dismay was on my side when, from the derisive smile with which they heard my decision, I realized that my bluff had failed. I fear that my gracious pardon extended to them the following morning hardly carried me through. Unable to get rid of them by sending them out of the island I had them relegated to a part of the harbour where it was unlikely they would meet me again. I had learnt my lesson.

March 28 brought with it the first evidences of enemy aero-activity, when the *Ark-Royal*, a kite balloon vessel, was attacked by aeroplanes. No damage was done and the next day we were ready with a reply, for our aerodrome was by that time established at Tenedos under the command of Commánder Samson, who brought with him a great reputation owing to the work he had done in Flanders.

" March 30, 1915. . . . Verily I believe that Lemnos is the original birthplace of all the winds. After a few days' peace we have another howling gale of wind to-day with the usual inconveniences attached, difficulties in communication, delay and unavoidable damage, it is the very deuce and all. . . .

" I think I have got over most of my worst difficulties, but certainly not with the assistance of the Admiralty. Like nearly all public departments they won't take any strong line to help their people. I am obliged of course to keep a very sharp eye on all persons arriving here, for on my shoulders rest the responsibility for the safety not only of the troops and ships but also of the civil population. Now since the agreement with Greece for our occupation of this place is secret, a secret which every one shares! and since my appointment is, so to speak, *sub rosa*, if I take any drastic measures towards securing this safety I may come up against the Greek authorities. For this I am quite prepared but naturally wish to be backed up by the authorities at home. But do you think they give me necessary assurances? Of course not. However I have diddled them all by managing to get the Greek authorities to *ask* me to take certain responsibilities.

" I needn't tell you that I am delighted with the results of my diplomacy and am now in the position of conferring a favour on the Greeks instead of them conferring a favour on me. . . . I am actually taxing the people who have come in and have set up booths, etc., and with the proceeds am taking certain very necessary sanitary measures which I trust the inhabitants will appreciate but which I am quite sure I do. . . . I sometimes look back to those happy days before the war and wonder whether we are in the same existence now as then. Truly the whole atmosphere of the world has altered; when will it ever calm down again? The end of hostilities will not, I fear, produce that result. . . . My staff now consist of eleven people, all of us as full of work as ever. It needn't have been half so hard had there been any sort of preparation at home. Amateur strategists and amateur warriors is what we are suffering from. . . . Everybody very cheery. . . .

" April 2, 1915. . . . The Greek authorities are now entirely acquiescent in my taking everything out of their hands. I don't think they could have dealt with the situation themselves, and I feel pretty certain that they must have had orders from Athens to at least put no obstacles in my way. . . . It is amusing to find oneself a sort of dictator, turning out whom one pleases, improving the condition of the inhabitants, substituting law and order for licence and chaos. I am on excellent terms with the French. . . ."

4

CHAPTER III

ON April 10 Sir Ian Hamilton, accompanied by the H.Q.S., returned from Egypt in the transport *Arcadian*, which also had on board General Hunter Weston, in command of the 29th Division, with whom in the very near future I was destined to be so closely associated.

The arrival of the G.H.Q. considerably reduced the difficulty of working out the combined plans which its separation from the Navy had hitherto rendered very real. Captain Mitchell had, as already related, been doing invaluable work with them in Egypt, and he now managed to obtain the assistance of twelve naval officers whom at my urgent request the Admiralty had sent out to act as Beach Masters.

Our means of dealing with repairs were also now happily enhanced by the arrival of the *Reliance*, a repair ship whose workshops proved invaluable, but better than all she had on board Engineer Captain Humphreys, whose resourcefulness, tact and ability were worth his weight in gold. Never during the ensuing months did he once fail to comply with the many and various demands made upon him, and the cheerful alacrity with which he dealt with all difficulties proved an invaluable asset.

The intricacy of the preparations required for disembarking an army of some 100,000 men, with guns, ammunition, stores of every kind, with no reserve of small craft and boats, in the face of an enemy, can be imagined.

The most careful organization was necessary for moving an armada of over 200 vessels with its accompaniment of lighters, pontoons, etc., out of the harbour to their stations. The very smallest detail had not only to be considered but to be embodied in orders, for on the two nights preceding the fateful morning the comparatively narrow waters separating Lemnos from the Peninsula would be alive with craft proceeding in more than one direction, and it was inevitable that the course of some should cross that of others. Since no vessel would be showing any lights the greatest care had to be exercised in timing their movements so as to prevent all chances of accidents. When it is remembered that all this had to be accomplished by a number of officers who had never worked together before, some idea may be gained of the complexity and magnitude of the task.

It was at this time we heard of the Russian Fleet having met the *Goeben* in the Black Sea. We had no particulars, but the only fact evident was that the latter had escaped and that she still had a speed of 23 knots, thus disposing of the many rumours anent her disablement which had been circulating.

As during the forthcoming attack General Hunter Weston and I were to act together at Helles in the same manner as were Admiral Thursby and General Birdwood in another locality, we were naturally thrown into continual intercourse. It was the first time I had ever been in such close collaboration with a General or he with an Admiral, and I look back with the greatest pleasure to that association

ripening into a firm friendship and an admiration
on my part for a gallant soldier to whose energy
and foresight were due so much of such success that
was eventually gained.

On April 13 we both embarked on board the
Dartmouth and after visiting the newly erected
aerodrome at Tenedos, made a reconnaissance of
the south coast of the Peninsula, going up the
Straits as far as Morto Bay. The enemy guns left
us severely alone and nothing could be seen of any
bodies of men, but there were very visible evidences
of increasing measures of defence—more entrenchments, barbed wire entanglements, etc. What he
saw satisfied the General, but I must confess that
when I remembered the gales of wind that had
prevailed for the last month and contemplated the
open anchorages in which our small craft would
have to lie, I devoutly hoped that the usual fine
weather to be expected in the Mediterranean after
the middle of April would not play us false.

The re-organized transports were now arriving
every day from Egypt—those containing the Royal
Naval Division assembling at Trebuki, where Captain Grant, H.M.S. *Canopus*, had a small squadron,
the remainder at Mudros. The route therefore
between Egypt and Mudros was a perpetual stream
of vessels sailing singly whose safety was ensured
by our command of the sea. The only danger arose
from the presence of some Turkish torpedo boats
reported to be at Smyrna, and to guard against this
peril that harbour was being watched by H.M.S.
Minerva and two destroyers, the *Wear* and the
Welland. On the night of the 15th one of the
torpedo boats, the *Deni Hissan*, slipped past our

watching ships, and early on the morning of the
16th gained the transport route near the island of
Skyros, and sighted the transport *Manitou,* carrying
a detachment of the 29th Division. The master of
the transport, never believing that the torpedo
boat could be other than British, paid no attention
until she hailed him, ordered him to stop and gave
him ten minutes to get the troops into the boats
before sinking her. The men were actually at
boat-drill at the time and a good deal of confusion
ensued. They began to get into and lower the boats
without orders, with the result that some were
capsized and fifty men drowned. The enemy fired
a torpedo which happily missed and then went off
in chase of another steamer, the *Osiris,* she had caught
sight of, but being unable to overhaul her she
returned to her first victim, fired a second torpedo,
equally abortive, and bolted.

On the *Canopus* receiving the S.O.S. from the
Manitou the destroyers *Kennet* and *Jed* were immediately sent after the enemy and were just coming
up with her off Cape Mastike when the destroyer
Wear was sighted ahead. The *Deni Hissar* thus
trapped ran herself ashore, the crew giving themselves up to the Greek commandant of the island,
by whom they were interned.

While the enemy was in this manner seeking to
attack our communications, we on our side were
endeavouring to assail his sea communications
between Constantinople and Gallipoli. With this
view Submarine E 15, Lieut.-Commander P. L.
Brodie, started on the morning of the 17th in an
attempt to pass through the Narrows into the Sea
of Marmora. Submerging at the entrance of the

Straits at early dawn, she must have been swept out
of her course by the current, for shortly afterwards
an aeroplane which had been following her passage
reported that she was aground close to Kephaz
Light and was being heavily fired upon by Fort
Dardanus. ¡The possibility of her falling into the
enemy's hands and being made use of by him against
us was a perturbing thought and Admiral de Robeck
determined that this should not be allowed to happen.   He sent two destroyers after dark to try and
recapture her, or not succeeding in this to destroy
her.   But the attempt failed, for the destroyers were
unable to locate her and were received with so
heavy a fire that they were obliged to return without
having attained their object.   On the following day
another submarine, D 11, made a further endeavour
and entered the Straits submerged with the object
of torpedoing the stranded vessel, but owing to a
thick fog was unable to do this.   The battleships
Triumph and *Majestic* were then ordered to try and
destroy her by gunfire, but they too were unsuccessful, being driven off by the enemy's shell fire before
they could get in range.   A fourth venture was
made by two picket boats from these ships.   Under
the command of Lieut.-Commander Robinson of the
Majestic and Lieutenant Godwin of the *Triumph*,
manned by volunteer crews, they crept up the
European shore under cover of night until they
believed themselves opposite the spot where E 15
lay.   It was pitch dark and they had nothing to
guide them except a boat's compass and their own
judgment.   As they hauled out from the European
shore and steamed across the Straits they were
caught by the beams of a search-light which until

that moment had not been operating and ran into heavy fire. However, the light which exposed their presence to the enemy also lighted up and showed them their target. Lieutenant Godwin immediately fired his torpedo and had no sooner done so than his boat was hit by a shell and began to sink rapidly. Lieut.-Commander Robinson, who also had fired his torpedo, in spite of the heavy fire they were under, went alongside the sinking boat and succeeded in transferring her crew to his before she sank and then steamed away at full speed without being hit. The next morning a reconnaissance by aeroplane showed that the task so gallantly undertaken had been successful, for E 15 was a complete wreck. This exploit, so worthy of the very highest of the Navy's traditions, was carried out with the loss of but one man. Lieut.-Commander Robinson was rewarded with the V.C. and Lieutenant Godwin with the D.S.O., and never were these decorations more worthily bestowed.

It was afterwards learned that Lieut.-Commander Brodie and six of his crew had been killed when the submarine ran aground and was fired on and that the remainder had been taken prisoner. By a pathetic coincidence Lieut.-Commander Brodie's twin brother, who was also serving in the Fleet, was an observer in the aeroplane that reported the destruction of his brother's vessel.

Since the arrival of Sir Ian Hamilton the work of completing the plans and orders had been pushed forward with as much speed as their amplitude and complexity would allow. Every ingenuity our resources permitted of had been applied to the transports to facilitate and quicken the disembarkation of the troops, and the troops themselves underwent as much boat-drill as time would admit of.

The object of the expedition was to capture the Kilid Bahr plateau on the Gallipoli Peninsula and thereby dominate the forts at the Narrows of the Straits. This also would entail destroying the enemy's concealed and mobile batteries.

The strength of the enemy was estimated at 40,000 men, and information pointed to a landing being opposed.

The general plan to achieve this object was :—

1st. A bombardment of the Bulair lines at daybreak by a portion of the Fleet on a given morning, followed by a feint of landing on the mainland north of the Xeros islands carried out by the transports of the Royal Naval Division.

2nd. A simultaneous bombardment of the heights commanding the beach between Gaba Tepe and Nibrunesi Point accompanied by a landing of the Australian and New Zealand Army Corps.

3rd. Simultaneously a bombardment of the southern extremity of the Peninsula accompanied by a landing of the 29th Division in the neighbourhood of Cape Helles.

At the same time the French Fleet would make a demonstration in combination with which was to be a landing near Kum-Kale by the French Expeditionary Force.

The covering forces for these landings consisted of one Brigade of the A.N.Z.A.C., one Field Company of R.E., and three Bearer Sub-Divisions for the landing at Gaba Tepe ; one Brigade and one Battalion of the 29th Division, one Field Company

of R.E. and three Bearer Sub-Divisions for the
landing at Cape Helles.

The disembarkation of the main bodies at Gaba
Tepe and Cape Helles was to commence directly
the covering forces had landed and seized the beaches.

The operations at Gaba Tepe to be carried out by
General Birdwood commanding the A.N.Z.A.C. in
conjunction with Rear-Admiral Thursby commanding
a division of the Fleet, those at Cape Helles by General
Hunter Weston commanding the 29th Division in
conjunction with myself commanding another division of the Fleet, with Rear-Admiral Stuart Nicholson as my second in command. The Plymouth
Battalion R.M.L.I. was to be at the disposal of the
General Officer Commanding in Chief (Sir Ian Hamilton) ready to be landed as circumstances required.

Two floating piers that my agent had procured
at the Piræus would be available for use on the
first day and trestle piers were to be commenced
at the earliest opportunity. Communications to
the Fleet were to be made through naval signal
stations established on shore, and naval signalmen
were to be landed with the covering force for this
purpose. It was hoped that casualty clearing
stations would be located on all the beaches by
the afternoon of the first day and 150 rounds of
ammunition per rifle and the same number of rounds
for gun ammunition, 1,000 rounds for each machine
gun and seven days' rations per man and horse
were to be landed during the first day. Sir Ian
Hamilton and the General Headquarters were to
be on board H.M.S. *Queen Elizabeth.*

The Fleet was organized in six squadrons, the
first squadron comprising the eight battleships

Swiftsure (flying the flag of Rear-Admiral Nicholson), *Albion, Lord Nelson, Implacable, Vengeance, Prince George, Goliath* and *Cornwallis* and the cruisers *Euryalus* (flying my flag), *Minerva, Talbot* and *Dublin* with six fleet-sweepers was to operate off Cape Helles under my command with the 29th Division. The second squadron consisted of the battleships *Queen* (flying the flag of Rear-Admiral Thursby), *London, Prince of Wales, Triumph* and *Majestic*, the cruiser *Bacchante*, eight destroyers and four trawlers. These were to co-operate off Gaba Tepe with A.N.Z.A.C.

The third squadron, under Captain H. S. Grant, H.M.S. *Canopus*, included the cruisers *Dartmouth* and *Doris* and two destroyers, and with the transports of the R.N. Division were to carry out the feint off Bulair. The fourth squadron, comprising the cruisers *Sapphire* and *Amethyst* and twelve trawlers, were to work with the first squadron ; and the fifth squadron, composed of the battleships *Agamemnon*, ten destroyers and some mine-sweepers, were to operate inside the entrance of the Straits under Captain Fyler of H.M.S. *Agamemnon*.

The sixth squadron was composed of the French ships under Contre-Amiral Guépratte and consisted of three battleships, the *Jauréguiberry* (flag), *Henri IV*, and *Charlemagne*, the cruisers *La Touche-Treville*, *Jeanne d'Arc, Savoie*, seven destroyers, five torpedo boats and the Russian cruiser *Askold*.

The first and second squadrons provided covering and attendant ships, the duties of the former being the bombardment of the positions and the covering of the landing, those of the latter, the carrying of the advance parties.

After much consideration a night operation, in spite of the possibilities of surprise it held out, was abandoned in favour of an attack at dawn. The difficulty—the improbability even—of the boats reaching the shore at the selected places in the dark, was deemed sufficient reason for this decision and was strengthened by the fear of the possible confusion that might arise from landing heavily equipped men in small boats during the night. It was therefore arranged that the attendant ships should convey the advanced parties as close to the shore as possible and embark them in their boats at earliest dawn.

The size of the advance parties was necessarily limited to the numbers the boats could carry and any method by which these numbers could be increased would have been welcome.

At a joint meeting of the Staffs, Commander Unwin put forward a proposal for landing a large number of men from a specially prepared ship which herself would be run ashore on the beach. He believed that if the landings were well defended and the enemy's fire reserved until the boats were close, but few of them would ever reach the shore at all, and his plan was conceived as a method of ensuring the troops being landed. The Staff did not view the proposal favourably ; they thought it entailed too great a risk, for if the ship were sunk before she reached her destination, the sacrifice in men would be too great. When the scheme was laid before me, however, I was at once attracted by the promise it held out of overcoming the disadvantage under which we were labouring from the shortage of boats for landing sufficiently large numbers of men at one time. Further examination convinced me that the risk of the ship being sunk was not so great as it appeared, and I was able to win over the military authorities to my views and the scheme was adopted with their full consent. It was an attractive idea reminiscent of the wooden horse of Troy. We hoped that after fulfilling her main function, the vessel would prove useful as a depôt, as a shelter where wounded might receive attention and as a pier from which, with her good derricks, guns and stores might be landed. She would carry a large amount of fresh water for immediate use and would be capable of condensing many tons a day.

The plan for disembarking the men was as follows : Eight ports were cut in her side, large enough to allow a fully equipped man to pass through to a temporary gallery rigged round the ship leading to the bows, from whence they would reach the shore over a steam hopper forming a bridge. This hopper was self-propelled and fitted with a brow to drop on the beach as soon as she took the shore. The hopper was towed alongside the ship and when the latter grounded, would proceed under her own steam to fill the gap between the ship's bows and the shore. Perfection would have been reached had her length been such as to entirely fill the gap, but as we did not know how the beach shelved, no exact calculations could be made and three wooden lighters were therefore also towed to make certain of completing the bridge. A suitable ship was found in the *River Clyde*, under charter to the French Government, that was immediately sent alongside the *Reliance* and prepared for the part she was to play. The work of fitting her out was entirely in the hands of Commander Unwin, to whom I gave the command. His call for volunteers to man the *River Clyde* met with a ready response from the crew of the *Hussar*, from whom he selected six seamen, six engine-room ratings and the ship's carpenter, with Midshipman Drewry, R.N.R., as second in command. When the list was complete : " a leading seaman named Williams," wrote Commander Unwin, " came up to me and asked if he could not come. I told him I was full up and that I did not want any more petty officers, to which he replied, ' I'll chuck my hook (meaning he would give up his rating) if you will let me come,' and I·did, to his cost but everlasting glory. I shall never forget the way he died."

By the 19th all was at length ready, the plans perfected, the arrangements completed, the orders issued and I transferred my flag to the *Euryalus* the same day. Little had I imagined when she had left my squadron at Plymouth only a few weeks before that I should so shortly find myself on board her under such totally different and more exciting circumstances. It was pleasant to be once more surrounded by officers and men whom I had grown to know so well during those weary months in the Channel and for whom I had formed so high a regard. That morning at a meeting on board the *Queen Elizabeth* it was decided that the attack should be delivered on the 23rd, and that the first movements must therefore commence on the 21st. There was one factor, however, upon which more than any other not only the success, but the actual realization of the project depended—the only factor over which we had no control—the weather. In that part of the Mediterranean, settled conditions may be generally expected after the middle of April and a study of records of many years had led to the conclusion that after the 14th light airs and smooth seas might almost be depended upon. Unfortunately a strong breeze sprang up on the morning of the 20th rendering it impossible that these dates should be adhered to. The following day (the one fixed for the first move) brought with it no improvement, and very reluctantly at noon a postponement was ordered. The bad weather continued until the evening of the 22nd and on the morning of Friday, 23rd, a steadily rising glass giving promise of the necessary favourable conditions, it was decided that the preliminary movements should be commenced that afternoon.

The first ships to leave were the three transports carrying the battalions forming the advance parties for Helles and Morto Bay, bound for an anchorage off Tenedos. They were shortly afterwards followed by the *Euryalus, Implacable, Cornwallis* and the *River Clyde.*

How different was the appearance of Mudros that day to its aspect two months before when I first arrived. Except for the fine outline of the distant hills the scenery is neither beautiful nor interesting though at evening the setting sun will occasionally change the pervading yellow into a soft pink. The hillsides sloping gradually down to the flat plain contiguous to the waters of the harbour are of unbroken monotony and bare of any vegetation except scrub, and convey a somewhat depressing idea of poverty, almost desolation. The little

town, then as uninteresting and devoid of anima-
tion as any of its many counterparts in the Grecian
Archipelago, was now teeming with life and activity ;
its one pier, then deserted except for an occasional
fishing boat, was now so crowded as to require
detailed organization for the regulation of the traffic.
The harbour, at that time almost empty, was now
crowded with vessels of every description, men of
war, hospital ships, tugs, lighters and pontoons,
calling to mind some busy centre such as Southampton or Liverpool, rather than a usually unfrequented harbour of an unimportant Greek island.
This heterogeneous mass of shipping would have
conveyed to the uninitiated eye an impression of
disorderly profusion, but was in fact one composite
whole, whose every unit was an organized integral
part, ready to move at a given moment to its assigned
station with full knowledge of the part it had to
play in the forthcoming struggle. So full was the
harbour that the French transports that had arrived
somewhat later than the English ones had been
obliged to find an anchorage in the outer roadstead.

My feelings as I stood on the bridge of the *Euryalus*
slowly steaming out to sea to meet the unknown
were those of confidence, hope and pride. The time
of uncertainty, of preparation and of waiting were
over. The hour of action had arrived and that
these stimulating thoughts pervaded the minds of
those thousands of men collected together in this
comparatively small space was clearly shown by the
enthusiasm which prevailed. Cheering bodies of
men must ever produce an exhilarating effect, and
when the cheers, as they did on this occasion, come
ringing over the water from troops on the eve of

action, from men about to take part in an undertaking
so desperate and fraught with such tremendous
issues, the impressions evoked cannot be otherwise
than emotional.

The sounds of the British cheering, dying away
as we receded from them, were taken up by our
French comrades in the outer roads, symbol of the
solidarity uniting the two nations. Passing close
to the *Jeanne d'Arc*, a French cruiser commanded
by Commandant, now Admiral, Grasset that had
formed one of the Channel Patrol, I signalled to
him : " This is better than the Channel " ; a message, he told me long afterwards, that had caught
the fancy of his ship's company who had received it
with fresh outbursts of cheers.

And so amidst spontaneous enthusiasm the expedition left Mudros and we spent a quiet night steaming
slowly to Tenedos, where we arrived early the
following morning.

Our object in going to this anchorage was two-
fold : it was to transfer the advance parties from
their transports to the attendant ships and to prepare the boats from which they were to rush the
beaches. These boats had to be towed to the rendezvous off Helles, and since there were ninety of them
the utmost care had to be exercised that there should
be nothing missing and that they should be in a
perfect state of preparation on our arrival at the
rendezvous. The anchorage of Tenedos was chosen
on account of being only half the distance from
Mudros to the Peninsula.

The weather once more caused grave anxiety.
During the night the wind had freshened and raised the
sea sufficiently to mar our plans should it continue.

Neither did it abate in the morning and I spent some harassing hours watching the glass and wondering if, after all, we should not again have to make a postponement. It was calculated that it would take at least six hours to accomplish all that had to be done and since on account of the number of open boats in tow the final passage to the rendezvous would have to be made at slow speed the start could not be later than 10 p.m. I felt that if after 2 p.m. there was no improvement there was nothing to be done except to wait until conditions were favourable and I should then have to communicate with the Vice-Admiral, with whom of course the final decision rested. But to think what a further postponement at the eleventh hour would mean! At the worst, the return of the whole expedition to Mudros—at the best, waiting where we were and giving the enemy a short indication of the approaching attack. Not that I had any illusions on that subject. It was incredible to me that he should not already know that we had started, for what was to prevent the news of our departure the day before reaching Kastro from Mudros and from Kastro being passed on to him? I had taken every precaution that was in my power but was, alas! only too conscious how illusory they were. At noon there appeared to my hopeful nature signs of the breeze dying away, but to be of any use the weather must have moderated sufficiently by 2 p.m. to make the possibility of the expedition starting a certainty —and then the luck changed and by 1.50 p.m. the wind had gone and with it the slight sea and the final preparations commenced.

In the course of the afternoon General Hunter

5

Weston and his staff took up their quarters on board the *Euryalus* preparatory to the attack, assuredly the first time that a General had ever commanded his division from the deck of a man-of-war. Indeed, the whole operation was altogether unprecedented and differed in every respect from any this generation of soldiers and sailors, at all events, had either known or taken part in.

Besides transferring the troops (some 6,000) from the transports to the attendant ships and to the *River Clyde*, the pulling boats, in which they were to gain the beaches, had to be prepared in such a manner that after having been towed during the night they would be in a complete state of readiness on reaching the rendezvous in the morning. The work was perfectly simple, but it was of the utmost importance that no detail, however slight, should be overlooked, for there would be no time to put matters right the next morning at the moment when the troops would be embarked and when so small a mistake might spell so great a disaster.

The squadron was organized in three divisions, each comprising one attendant ship, two fleet-sweepers, two trawlers and a flotilla of sixteen steam-pinnaces and thirty pulling boats, each of these flotillas being in their turn divided into six tows consisting of one steam pinnace and five pulling boats each. The attendant ship towed two tows and each sweeper and trawler one, and in this formation, under a setting moon with a smooth sea, the squadron steamed at slow speed in the direction of the Peninsula towards the great adventure.

"April 23. . . . I begin this letter in peace and quiet on board my old *Euryalus*. I wonder what I shall have to tell you before I end it. All these last weeks we have been preparing and organizing for landing the army on the Gallipoli Peninsula and now here I am on my way over from Lemnos to Tenedos, the first stage of the operation, and to-morrow night we leave Tenedos to attack on Sunday morning. The scheme is audaciously bold and I think we have done all we can to help to make it a success. But the authorities at home! They seem to think it is a picnic party for all the assistance they have given us. Of course the initial mistake was bombarding (the forts) before we had an army to land. Had we had troops to pour in after the first bombardment the whole thing would have been finished and done with in a very short time. But we hadn't. Then this hastily devised plan of sending troops out to Mudros without any organization or people to do it. The whole of the transports had to be unpacked and re-packed again, then the whole thing had to be re-organized out here and I had no staff. By beseeching and telegraphing I got twelve officers out from England and we should have had fifty—and all in the same proportion. However that part of it is finished and now we are going to utilize what we have created. But alas! we have given the Turks, or rather the Germans, time to prepare and the landing will be a very different thing now to what it would have been a month ago. We have 18,000 regular troops, splendid—over 30,000 Australians, splendid material, but their worth has yet to be proved, 18,000 to 20,000 French troops and about 15,000 Winston's Army—in all, from 80,000 to 85,000 men. Never in the history of the world has such an expedition sailed, never has a big campaign been so hastily organized and got together and never has such an undertaking had so little consideration given it from home. I believe we shall succeed simply because every one is determined that it must. There is no other alternative. Certainly the Generals are full of dash and determination and everybody, naval and military, is full of the right sort of spirit. Sunday will be a wonderful day but we *must* have fine weather. To-night I feel a great load off my shoulders, the hard thinking work is over and finished and to-morrow morning I shall be as fit as a lark. Well, the army once landed we then have to finish the Dardanelles forts, a comparatively easy job with the troops on shore to help us, and then for Constantinople. . . . In the meantime my work is extraordinarily varied. I am still Governor of Mudros where I have left a locum tenens *pro tem.* landing or hoping to land the army, organizing supplies for the troops and besides this commanding a squadron from this ship—truly a multifarious business. It is wonderful experience, but I have good fellows all around me and they all do well. We want just a little bit of luck and we shall make history. . . ."

CHAPTER IV

THE night passed without incident, the slumbering forms of the soldiers on the upper deck being the only sign of anything unusual taking place. At 4 a.m., when still quite dark, the ship was stopped, the boats came alongside, and the troops entered them without the slightest confusion and in the deepest silence. So quietly indeed was the embarkation carried out, that the impression conveyed was that of a phantom force. The steam pinnaces with their five pulling boats in tow then formed up in line abreast and began to steam towards the shore, the *Euryalus* keeping in line with them.

As dawn began to break, forms hitherto invisible commenced little by little to reveal themselves, the boats full of men to assume a more definite shape, the outlines of the coast to show up against the slowly lightening eastern sky and the men of war, that during the night had taken up their positions ready for bombarding, to loom out from the vanishing darkness. Suddenly—at 5.15 a.m.—the profound stillness of the awakening day was broken by the sound of a gun and instantly the whole fleet burst into a roar of fire. The bombardment continued until the boats were close to the beach, when it had to be stopped for fear of hitting our own men. Under its cover the steam pinnaces with their tows made straight for the shore. Owing to the current

proving stronger than anticipated we passed the
Swiftsure and the *Albion* stationed off W and V
Beaches respectively about fifteen minutes after
the appointed time, and when about 1,000 yards
from the shore, the *Euryalus* stopped and joined in
the bombardment, the tows continuing at full speed
to make for the now clearly defined beaches. When
as close in as they could get without grounding the
steam pinnaces slipped the tows and the pulling
boats, coming up in line abreast, pushed on under
oars until they took the ground. Up to this moment
the fire of our ships had prevented the enemy from
leaving his dug-outs, but immediately it ceased a
hail of rifle and machine gun fire opened upon the
attacking party who, jumping out of the boats,
found themselves struggling in wire-entanglements
which the ships' guns had failed to destroy. To us,
standing on the bridge of the *Euryalus* eagerly
watching every movement through our glasses, the
situation appeared desperate. The leading men as
they jumped ashore were shot down and lay huddled
on the entanglement, forming a human hedge over
which their comrades from behind passed, only in
their turn to be shot down. Fortunately the left
hand tows, making for some rocks at the point
where the beach ended and the sloping ground
began, were not subjected to so deadly a fire and
landing with but slight loss captured a position
enfilading the beach. The ships, too, after locating
the positions the enemy were firing from, again
took up the bombardment, the projectiles passing
close over the heads of our men who, undeterred
by their losses, eventually got through the wire and
began to form up under the rising ground.

The emotions evoked by the incidents of those few but seemingly endless minutes are difficult to describe ; a wild hope as our boats approached the beach, whilst still the enemy held his fire, that perhaps after all the landing was going to be effected without resistance ; then, almost before this thought had taken shape, its shattering by the sudden roar of musketry ; the feeling of sickening horror as our men were seen to fall motionless on the wire ; and finally the dread shadow of failure, already beginning to obtrude itself, gradually giving way to the triumphant conviction that nothing could stop the British soldier and that the beach was won !

Away on our left, too far off for us on board the *Euryalus* to see what was happening, the *Implacable* was landing her troops at X Beach in a similar manner, but under somewhat different circumstances.

There the enemy, instead of waiting until the boats reached the shore, opened fire as soon as they were in range, and Captain Lockyer, handling his ship in a masterly manner, eased down his anchor until it was hanging with two shackles of cable out and steamed slowly on until brought up by it. This occurred between 400 and 500 yards from the shore, and from this position, broadside on, he poured a volume of fire from his 12-inch and 6-inch guns upon the ridges from which the enemy's fire proceeded. Under this intense bombardment, kept up till the whole force was on shore, the boats advanced and the troops were landed without casualty.

The third of the covering ships, the *Cornwallis*, had a somewhat different rôle to fulfil.

Morto Bay, just inside the entrance of the Straits, had, after much consideration, been judged unsuitable for landing any considerable numbers of troops on account of the reefs known to obstruct its entrance and of the strong defence afforded to it by the guns of the Asiatic shore. General Hunter Weston, however, attached much 'importance to landing a small force here for the protection of our right flank, and for this purpose three companies of 2nd South Wales Borderers had been detailed, the landing to be covered by the *Cornwallis*. Directly this ship had seen the party safely ashore she was to join the *Albion* and assist in covering the landing on V Beach.

Of all the landings this one at Morto Bay was that which had caused me the most anxiety. I feared that the hindrances bound to be encountered through navigational troubles and the fire from both shores would render it the one most difficult of accomplishment. Whilst still at Tenedos therefore, I had told Captain Davidson of the *Cornwallis* that before joining the *Albion* he was to stay and support these troops, rendering them such assistance as he could until they had effected a landing.

Like those on board the *Euryalus* and *Implacable*, these men were embarked in their boats from the *Cornwallis* outside the Straits at 4 a.m.; but unfortunately every available naval steamboat had been absorbed elsewhere and they had to be towed by trawlers; but trawlers are slow, and, moreover, they encountered the full strength of the current sweeping out of the Straits and in consequence did not reach their destination until 7.30 a.m., when the trawlers took the ground about 400 yards from the beaches. During the passage up to Morto Bay, the boats were screened from observation from the

European shore by the *Cornwallis*, but encountered severe shell-fire from the Asiatic batteries, in spite of the bombardment that these batteries themselves were undergoing at the hands of the *Lord Nelson* and the *Vengeance*, stationed inside the Straits for this purpose. However, the boats sustained no casualties and after the trawlers struck the pulling boats continued their way under oars without further opposition until they reached the beach, when they were met by heavy rifle-fire from the trenches commanding it. Of the three companies comprising the party, one landed and seized De Tott's Battery, while the other two, landing on the beach further inside the bay, rushed and captured the trenches.

Captain Davidson thought he could not better promote my wishes than by landing some bluejackets to help the disembarkation and by strengthening the attackers by a party of his marines. Immediately the trawlers were brought up he anchored his ship and not only sent his own men to the beach but, urged on by his own gallantry, accompanied them himself and reached the shore in time to assist in taking the trenches. By 8.30 a.m. the position was in our hands with the loss of only a few casualties; and thus was the beach, regarded by me as presenting the most difficulty, captured the most easily.

Whilst initial success was being won at Morto Bay and at W and X Beaches, a serious check was encountered at V Beach. Rather longer than W, it runs in a gentle curve from the bluff at Cape Helles to the old fort at Sedd-el-Bahr behind which lies the village of that name. The land slopes down to the beach in varying inclines, steep near the extremities,

more gentle in the centre, forming a natural amphitheatre from any part of which the whole beach can
be commanded ; it was therefore admirably suited
to defence. The enemy had taken full advantage
of these features. The beach itself, as at W, was
wired right down to the water edge, the fort and
village filled with cunningly concealed machine
guns and the slopes entrenched up to the old Castle,
frowning down upon the sea from a height of some
150 feet.

The plan of attack here was on the same lines as
at W and X Beaches, but the numbers were increased
by the 2,000 men in the *River Clyde*.

The troops for this attack, other than those in the
River Clyde, had been conveyed from Tenedos in
fleet-sweepers and like the others been transferred to
boats at 4 a.m. These boats, too, were behind their
time, and it was 6.40 a.m. when the steam boats
slipped their tows and the boats began to pull the
short remaining distance to the shore. Until this
moment the *Albion* had been bombarding the beach
and the surrounding amphitheatre, but, alas ! with
no better success than the *Swiftsure* had obtained
at W. The moment therefore she ceased bombarding, the boats were subjected to a furious storm of
fire before they even reached the land ; indeed,
but very few did reach it. The majority of them
were disabled and were to be seen drifting help-
lessly about, full of killed and wounded. There was
one which had in it not a living man ; another
entirely disappeared. It was a horrible sight, and
all the worse because of the inability to render
effectual aid. Only a mere handful of men who,
somehow or other, had reached the beach, found

shelter under a ridge where the land began to rise. This part of the attack was, in fact, wiped out before it commenced and on the *River Clyde* rested the only chance of gaining a footing.

The story of the *River Clyde* contains incidents of heroism sufficient to form an epic in itself. It is without parallel in the history of warfare, and the bravery and courage there exhibited has rarely been equalled and never surpassed. It is hardly an exaggeration to say that to those gallant souls, soldiers and sailors, who manned her, is principally due the achievement of our having gained a foothold on the Peninsula.

She, like the other ships, had completed her arrangements when lying off Tenedos the day before, and had left that anchorage at the same time as, but independently of, the remainder of the squadron, with orders that the ship should be beached immediately after the first boats had reached the shore. But at daybreak, when in a position to make for the beach, Commander Unwin found that the boats he was to follow were behind their time, and since he did not dare stop his engines to await them for fear of fouling his propeller with the lighters towing astern, he was obliged to turn round and make a detour, no easy matter with the hundreds of boats and vessels surrounding him. Once round, however, and his bow pointed for the shore, he went full speed ahead. On came the *River Clyde* through a storm of fire from both European and Asiatic batteries. She was hit several times, but sustained no material damage, though a few men were killed, but her Commander's nerve and steady hand never failed him and the vessel took the ground at 6.30 a.m. in her assigned position, but, unfortunately, further out than had been hoped owing to the beach being more shelving than expected.

Directly she touched, Commander Unwin rushed to the side and was horrified to see that the hopper, instead of going ahead as intended, was hung up alongside. It was only a long time afterwards that it was ascertained that her engines had been stopped before the *River Clyde* touched and that she consequently was pulled up at the same time, kept back by the towing line which did not slacken. When at last this was cleared and the hopper free, the latter was struck by a gust of wind as she forged ahead, and swinging away failed to place herself between the ship and the shore. The wooden lighters, however, shot ahead, and Commander Unwin, realizing the possible results of the failure of the hopper to fulfil her part, with no other thought than the success of the enterprise, jumped into the lighter and with the assistance of Lieutenant Morse, R.N., Midshipmen Malleson, R.N., and Drewry, R.N.R., Petty Officers Russell and Rummings and Able Seamen Williams and Samson got them into position under the ship's bows and, standing up to their waists in water, held them in position whilst the troops began to pour out of the ship, only to be received by a murderous fire from hundreds of rifles and machine guns. For more than an hour did these devoted men, the targets of this concentrated fire, continue their work of keeping the lighters in position and attempting to secure them. They seemed to bear charmed lives, for whilst all around them were falling, they stuck to their task until the bridge had been established ; and then, just as their labours were finished, Williams was struck by a

6-inch shell, and Commander Unwin, who was standing beside him, caught him as he fell and with the assistance of Midshipman Drewry, was carrying him back to the ship when he, Commander Unwin, lost consciousness and remembered no more, until about an hour later he found himself in his bunk, wrapped up in blankets with the doctor standing over him. Whilst he was lying there, Midshipman Drewry was brought in, slightly wounded by a bullet that had grazed his forehead, but after having it bound up, he was enabled to return to his work.

It was not long before Commander Unwin was up and about again. Dressed in a white shirt and flannel trousers—he had no longer a uniform to put on—he went into the hopper to see if anything could be done to ameliorate the situation. She was a veritable shambles—not of troops from the *River Clyde*, but of men who had attempted to land from the boats and had been turned back by the shouts and warnings of the very few of their comrades who had effected a landing and were now huddled under the ridges at the edge of the beach. He had not been in the hopper 'more than a few minutes when a bullet struck a stanchion close to him, spattering his face and neck with débris. Thus seeing that nothing further could be done and that the men lying there were all dead, he struggled back to the ship, assisted by a man who was shot through the lungs whilst doing so.

It was now realized that there was no use in trying to land any more men, for to cross the lighters was certain death. Colonel Carrington Smith, commanding the troops on board, therefore gave orders to stop the disembarkation. At that moment a party of British troops was seen trying to make its way from W Beach with the object of outflanking the enemy defending V Beach. Cheering on these men, 'a cheer taken up by the troops on board, the Colonel followed Commander Unwin to the bridge, but while the latter reached the upper bridge, the Colonel paused on the lower one, which had no protection, looking towards the shore through his glasses. Commander Unwin, turning round to warn him of his danger, saw Colonel Carrington Smith fall down dead, shot through the mouth.

For the present, at all events, there was no more to be done and Commander Unwin remained on the bridge in company with Colonel Williams and Colonel Doughty Wylie. The latter, a remarkable man who had already distinguished himself years before during massacres at Aleppo, was now a member of the Intelligence Department of the Staff and had joined the troops on board the *River Clyde* of his own initiative.

The prospect on board the *River Clyde* throughout that weary day was not encouraging. The troops were subjected to trials as severe as can ever have fallen to the lot of a soldier. They were crowded into a ship to emerge from which was certain death; they were unaware of all that was happening around them; the ship sheltering them was already the target of many machine guns and might at any moment be hit by heavy shells; but owing to the fine spirit of leadership displayed by the officers of those splendid regiments and to the feeling of confidence in them that pervaded the men, a perfect state of discipline was maintained that not only enabled them to pass through the ordeal unscathed, but allowed them to perform a feat of arms the following morning which went far towards effecting the success of the landing.

The beach to the right and left was strewn with dead. Under the ridges, but a few yards inland, were crouching small parties of men unable to move. Six of them tried at one time to move out with the evident intention of cutting the wire entanglements ; five of them were shot down before they could get ten yards, the sixth ran back and jumping over the heads of the men lying under the ridges, regained his shelter.

At about 2 p.m. the moaning of some wounded men lying on a reef under the vessel's starboard bow, induced Commander Unwin to make an attempt to get them on board. Getting into a pinnace whose stern he connected to the ship by a rope, he punted himself over to the reef and after having cut off their accoutrements, lifted seven of them into the pinnace, placing some of them on his back and crawling along the reef on his hands and knees. He was joined by a man of the R.N.A.S. named Russell, who, inspired by Unwin's example, had swum out to assist him in his work of mercy. As together they were lifting a man into the boat, Russell was hit in the stomach by a bullet. Unwin tore off a part of his shirt, bound up the wound and got him into the boat, but his strength by this time was spent. He could do no more, and so he had himself and the wounded men hauled on board. His labour of rescue was, however, continued by a young officer, Tizzard, killed a fortnight afterwards, but not before he had been recommended for the V.C. awarded to him posthumously.

The situation of the ship and her devoted crew
had not been rendered any the better from the reported presence of a party of our men in the village
of Sedd-el-Bahr, making it impossible for the *Albion*
to open fire on it. These men had landed in the
boat camber just to the eastwards of where the *River
Clyde* was beached from the two right-hand tows and
had penetrated into the village without opposition.
But when they tried to push on, they were met by
such heavy fire from machine guns concealed in the
houses, that progress was impossible and after heavy
losses their remnants had to be re-embarked. At
this time the *Queen Elizabeth*, having on board Sir
Ian Hamilton and Admiral de Robeck, who had been
watching the landing of the Australians at Gaba
Tepe, arrived on the scene of action and learning
that these men had been withdrawn immediately
opened fire with her 15-inch guns upon the fort and
villages, thus helping to relieve the situation created
by the absence of the *Cornwallis*, which had not yet
arrived from Morto Bay.

She, it will be remembered, was to have joined
the *Albion* as soon as the landing at Morto Bay had
been effected, and since I was aware that this had
already happened and that De Tott's Battery was in
our hands, her inexplicable delay was causing me
great anxiety. My signals to her were without
response and my annoyance proportionately great.
Little did I imagine that her gallant captain had
himself landed and was helping to storm the
trenches! The decision to divert the troops from
V to W Beach and to make no further attempt to
land the troops from the *River Clyde* until after dark
had already been taken by the time the *Cornwallis*

eventually did appear and she and the *Albion* were fully engaged for the remainder of the day helping to keep down the enemy's fire on the *River Clyde*, which in spite of her precarious situation proved a refuge for the remainder of her forces.

In the meantime, at W Beach the work of putting troops ashore had never ceased, and as the original party were reinforced they pushed their way up the slopes assisted by the guns of the *Euryalus* and the *Swiftsure* ; the shooting of the latter was particularly accurate and it was beautiful to watch from such a short distance the manner she burst her shells just beyond our men.

With the exception of the fatal V Beach where the troops in the *River Clyde* were still unable to leave the ship, the covering force was all on shore, and had gained the first positions by 9 a.m. The losses had been very heavy, but those wonderful troops had actually accomplished what many had believed to be an impossibility.

Although on board the *Euryalus* we knew that the party at Y Beach had landed without opposition, we had no information of their subsequent movements, but about 10 a.m. General Hunter Weston received a proposal from Sir Ian Hamilton that the troops diverted from V Beach should be landed to reinforce those at Y. Captain Dent, the principal naval transport officer, pointed out how such a change would involve considerable alteration in the original plans for landing guns, stores, etc., and after consulting with me the General came to the conclusion that the delay inevitably arising from such a change would be greater than he could afford and he adhered to his decision of putting these men

6

on to W Beach whose proximity to their original destination would not create any such dislocation of arrangements.

With the object of preventing any of the enemy forces located on the Asiatic side of the Straits being sent across to reinforce those at Helles a landing was made at Kum-Kale. This operation, never intended to be of an extended nature, but only as a diversion, was entrusted to the French forces under the command of General d'Amade. Directly a foothold had been obtained on the Peninsula they were to be re-embarked and brought over to the European shore to reinforce the troops that had already landed there.

The French transports, with their men of war, the *Jauréguiberry*, *Jeanne d'Arc* and *Henri IV*, to which were attached the British battleship *Prince George* and the Russian cruiser *Askold*, assembled in the roadstead outside Mudros Harbour on the morning of the 24th, and after General d'Amade had established his Headquarters on board the *Jauréguiberry* sailed at 10 p.m. the same evening for the entrance of the Straits, shaping a course to the southward of Tenedos in order to avoid the numerous other vessels that were at the same time making towards Helles.

A reconnaissance, made in a torpedo boat a few days before, had decided the General to throw his troops ashore on that part of the beach close to the northern salient of the old Fort of Kum-Kale, as it afforded some shelter to the disembarking troops from the machine guns in the Fort. The men-of-war and the five transports carrying the colonial regiment and battery of field artillery that were to make the attack arrived off the selected beach at

4.15 a.m. on the morning of the 25th, just as all the other troops from the British men-of-war were getting into their boat. The remainder of the French transports with the *Jeanne d'Arc* and five torpedo boats proceeded to Besika Bay where they made a feint of landing.

The disembarkation commenced at 7 a.m. covered by a heavy fire from the men-of-war, but the approach to the shore proved slow and difficult owing to the strong current. The first line of boats, in tow of the *Askold's* steam pinnace, owing to a mistake on the part of the officer in charge, instead of making for the selected spot, steamed towards an old wooden pier to the eastward. They encountered very heavy machine-gun fire, and one pinnace was sunk whilst the other boats found themselves adrift. They were, however, quickly picked up by other steam boats and conveyed to the proper place of disembarkation. The other tows, making for the eastern end of the beach, also came under a severe fire, but the Senegalese troops, gallantly led by their officers, jumped into the water with much dash and succeeded in capturing the old Fort, and thus gained comparative security for the remainder of the disembarkation.

But though the men-of-war subjected all the possible entrenched positions of the enemy to an intense bombardment the advance of the troops proved difficult. By 11 a.m., however, the whole of the village of Kum-Kale was in the possession of the French, but they were held up on the east by bodies of the enemy on the right bank of the Meander, and on the south by parties occupying the long ridge running from Yeni Sheir to the cemetery.

The second echelon was landed by 11.30 a.m. and from that time on there was a constant stream of boats backwards and forwards between the shore and the transport anchored a mile off.

It had been the General's original intention only to land the battery of 75's when the village of Yeni Sheir had been occupied, but owing to the strong resistance with which the cemetery was defended he decided to do so without waiting for this, and by 5 p.m. the whole of the 6th Regiment of the Colonial Brigade, with one battery, were on shore—some 2,800 men in all—under the command of Colonel Rueff—but they were confronted by a greatly superior force of the enemy, and at 6 p.m. orders were given for the troops to dig themselves in.

Four strong attacks, preceded by artillery fire, were delivered against the French front during the night, but were all beaten off with the assistance of the ships' guns.

Orders were given for the attack to be renewed at daylight on the following morning (26th), but at 7 a.m. General d'Amade, who had in the meantime landed, gave orders that the advance should be stopped, for he had come to the conclusion that the positions gained could only be held if the village of Yeni Sheir, situated on high ground, were occupied, and this could not be accomplished without using the whole of the French forces, which neither he nor Sir Ian Hamilton desired. General d'Amade went on board the *Queen Elizabeth* at 1.45 p.m. to explain the situation to Sir Ian and the order for withdrawal was given, though both Admiral de Robeck and Admiral Guépratte were anxious that the positions should be held for another twenty-four hours.

During the afternoon of the 26th, numbers of the enemy gave themselves up, and the situation improved so that an advance could have been made without much difficulty, but Colonel Rueff, having been informed that the troops would be re-embarked during the night, suspended all offensive operations.

By 7 p.m. Colonel Rueff had issued all the instruction for the withdrawal, and Admiral Guépratte had taken the necessary steps for the men-of-war transports and boats, and the movement commenced as soon as it was dark. A heavy fire was maintained on the enemy's positions, on which the searchlights of the squadron were thrown, by the ships' guns, and under cover of this bombardment the re-embarkation was successfully carried out. By 2 a.m. all the troops except a covering echelon of 700 men were once more on board their transports and these, together with 500 prisoners, were afloat by 5 a.m.

Thus was brought to a close an operation gallantly and successfully carried out under great difficulties, not the least of which was the shortage of boats that made it impossible for our gallant allies to land any large number of men at a time, and caused the disembarkation to take longer than otherwise would have been the case. It succeeded in fulfilling its purpose of containing a large number of the enemy and preventing their being reinforced on the Peninsula, and thus materially helped towards the success of the landing. The loss entailed was 54 officers and 567 men, killed, wounded, and missing.

This diversion had proved of considerable assistance to the attack on Helles by attracting to itself much of the enemy's fire, and by noon (25th) the situation on the Peninsula, though still terribly pre-

carious, had assumed a somewhat more stabilized
aspect. At Morto Bay and at Y Beach, though no
junction had been effected with the main body, the
forces were not being pressed ; those at X and W
Beaches had joined hands and on their right the
Lancashire Fusiliers were attempting to push out
with a view to capturing the trenches on the summit
of Cape Helles which commanded the beach and the
River Clyde. But the whole of the ground between
the two beaches had been wired and was covered
by machine guns in the ruins of Fort No. 1, and the
attempt proved impossible of accomplishment even
by the splendid Lancashire Fusiliers. As the afternoon wore on the exhausted troops could do no
more ; as it was, their efforts had been superhuman.
Our line was believed to reach unbroken from Y to
Helles, though, as we found later on, the junction
between X and Y had not been achieved. But the
position at Morto Bay, isolated as our troops there
were, caused anxiety. We had no reserves where-
with to reinforce them and all that could be done
was to station two battleships to render them all
assistance possible during the night.

I had told General Hunter Weston that the whole
of the 13,000 infantry would be landed by 3 p.m.
Several times during the day he had asked me
whether it were not possible to hasten the disembarkation, for every minute's delay made it more
difficult for him to gain his objective, Achi-Baba,
that evening. Though the work was being most
wonderfully performed, I dared not give him any
encouragement to hope for anything quicker, but
the task was eventually carried out in one hour less
than we had calculated.

Whilst the disembarkation was taking place with initial success at the southern extremity of the Peninsula a landing was being effected with much difficulty and in the face of equally strong opposition at Gaba Tepe where the attack had preceded the southern one by two hours. In Admiral Thursby's own words : " It was a bright clear night with a brilliant moon which did not set till 3 a.m. The ships were in line abreast, those with troops in the centre, the covering ships on the wings. The *Bacchante's* light (she had been sent on ahead to indicate the position) was sighted at 1 a.m. on Sunday morning. Soon afterwards the ships were stopped and the boats hoisted out, while the troops were given a good hot meal and a tot of grog. It was a perfectly still night with hardly a breath of wind, every sound was magnified, so much so that it seemed impossible that the noise of the boat-hoist engines could not be heard for miles away. We eagerly scanned the direction of the shore, the loom of which could just be seen, to see if we could detect any movement, but all was still. At last all the boats were in the water and orders given for the troops to be placed in them. This was carried out so quietly and expeditiously that I did not realize it had begun and sent to know what was the delay. My flag-lieutenant soon returned and informed me that nearly half the men were in the boats. I would not have believed that the operation could have been carried out so quietly that I could not hear them, although on the bridge only a few yards away. No higher testimony of the efficiency and discipline of these untried Australian and New Zealand troops is possible. As soon as all the ships had reported by wireless that all the men were embarked, the whole force proceeded slowly in the direction of the landing place, the *Queen*, *London* and *Prince of Wales*, each towing two long lines of boats, one on each quarter, the destroyers who had previously joined us following close astern. The moon had now set and it was dark and clear. When about two miles from the shore, engines were stopped and as the ships gradually lost their way, the lines of boats towed by picket-boats went ahead and gradually disappeared in the darkness and morning mist.

"Then came a period of waiting. It was the most nerve-racking twenty minutes I ever remember; the tension was tremendous. Suddenly a faint sound of rifle firing was heard and I knew the beach had been reached. I immediately signalled the destroyers to advance, and in they dashed at full speed. Dawn was now breaking and we could gradually make out white patches which were our boats on the beach; one or two on the left seemed wrecked and broken to pieces. Howitzers and field guns were now pouring in a hot fire and shells seemed to be coming from every direction. As the light increased the position could be more clearly defined; the men had landed from the destroyers and were dashing up the slopes to join their comrades who were already well up the hills. The noise made by rifle and machine-gun fire was growing in volume, punctuated by the louder explosions of shells from the heavy guns. The destroyers had stood in until their keels nearly touched the beach and so rapidly had the disembarkation proceeded that 4,000 men had been thrown ashore on a front of over a mile in just over half an hour.

"The rapidity with which such a large force had been landed undoubtedly saved the situation and had enabled our men to establish themselves on the high ground overlooking the beach in spite of all opposition !

"It was now 4.45 a.m. and the first four transports arrived on the scene and the disembarkation of the main body commenced. This operation was somewhat delayed as the transports could not take up their positions on account of the heavy fire brought to bear on them by some Turkish battleships in the Narrows at Kilia Leman. They were, however, soon driven off by our covering ships, but guns on Gaba Tepe also gave some trouble and were raking the beach. The *Bacchante* closed and anchored close in and in half an hour had completely silenced the guns. The disembarkation then proceeded and with such success that in spite of all difficulties some 8,000 men had been landed by 7 a.m.

"The landing had taken place practically as arranged, our right flank being only a hundred yards or so to the north of its assigned position. This was an advantage as it turned out, as it was found impossible to advance from the open beach and all our troops had to close in, so as to get the protection of the high ground.

"The beach under the high ground was so narrow and exposed to such a continuous fire that our beach parties found it impossible to organize it as arranged. The troops were unable to form up before advancing ; the men simply jumped out of the boats, threw aside all impedimenta and dashed, rifle and bayonet in hand, straight for the fighting line in front of them. The fight swayed backward and forwards, the Turks bringing up reinforcements as fast as we landed our men. Sometimes we made ground, sometimes we had to give way, so that from the sea our front appeared to be in an irregular line made up by groups of independent fights isolated from each other. Our covering ships did good service by keeping down the fire of the enemy's guns, firing up the ravines on either flank, clearing the tops of the hills, driving away the ships from the Narrows and supporting the fighting line. Meanwhile the landing of troops continued under heavy fire and the fight went on till dark without a definite decision being gained.

"The question of the disposal of the wounded became pressing. The hospital ship was filled up to her full capacity by 8.30 a.m. and had sailed for Alexandria. The transports detailed as hospital carriers had not been cleared of their troops and stores, and their medical officers and equipment were in the ship which had not yet arrived. In the meantime, the wounded were pouring in and had to be disposed of somehow; before dark there must have been 1,500 or more. The army medical staff on shore did wonders; it consisted only of a portion of one casualty clearing station. They never spared themselves and displayed the utmost gallantry in attending to the wounded under fire. It was quite impossible to keep the wounded on shore, exposed to a murderous fire, so they were put onto the boats that had landed the troops and taken back to the transports. In many cases the wounded were being hoisted up on one side while troops were being disembarked on the other. Captain Armstrong went round collecting as many as he could and sent them on board the *London* and other warships and arranged for others to be temporarily attended to until other hospital ships could be got ready, but I am afraid many of them had a very bad time that night.

"About 9 p.m. (the 25th) a message came to General Birdwood, who was on board the *Queen*, to say that his presence was necessary on shore. Before he landed, I arranged with him to keep Brig.-General Carruthers, his D.A. and Q.M.G. and Brig.-General Cunliffe Owen, his artillery officer, on board for the present as, until the position was thoroughly established on shore, the *Queen* was the best place from which to direct the landing operations and I could arrange with them all details as regards the disembarkation of men and stores and could co-ordinate the fire of the Fleet to meet the requirements of the troops on shore. I also arranged with him to disembark the New Zealand Corps and some guns during the night.

"At about 11 p.m. Captain Vyvyan, R.N., the Beach Master, came off to see me. He seemed rather agitated and said he had an important letter to give me from General Birdwood. In the letter he said that his Divisional Generals advised him that they did not think it possible for them to maintain their positions on shore, and that if the troops had to be re-embarked, the sooner it could be done the better. Captain Vyvyan further informed me that he had sent messages to the transports to send in their boats. I was quite taken aback, for I had no idea that things were in such a critical state on shore. A moment's consideration convinced me that to re-embark under such conditions would be disastrous and could not be thought of, especially as we did not yet know what had happened at Helles. The night had turned dark and stormy, our men were tired and disorganized, the confusion in any attempt to re-embark would have been indescribable and our losses must have been appalling. Besides which, I felt quite confident that when daylight came, I could, with the guns of the Fleet, hold back the enemy, while our men dug themselves in and re-organized, either for a further effort to advance or for an orderly re-embarkation under the guns of the Fleet.

"I at once countermanded the order for the boats to be sent on shore and told Captain Vyvyan I would go on shore at once and see General Birdwood and tell him of my decision. I asked Generals Carruthers and Cunliffe Owen to come on shore with me to see what arrangements we could make, naval or otherwise, to enable our men to hold on to the positions they had gained. We had just got into a steam-boat and were proceeding towards the beach when the officer of the watch hailed me and said that the *Queen Elizabeth* was standing towards us. I knew that both Admiral de Robeck and General Sir Ian Hamilton were on board her, so I went to her to report the situation. On arriving on board I had my first news of the southern landing which, so far, had only been partially successful. I sent General Birdwood's letter in to Sir Ian, who was in his cabin; he immediately came out and held a hurried Council of War during which he asked me for my opinion, which I gave and further told him that I was on my way on shore to see General Birdwood, and if he would give me a letter to him, I would deliver it personally and would explain to him the necessity of holding on at all costs. I was

soon down in my boat again with the letter from Sir
Ian and making for the shore, the position of which
could only be made out by the flashes from the rifles
and explosive shells. It was pitch dark, so we
stood in until we could see the white breakers and
hear the noise of the surf. It looked as if it would
be impossible to land in the steam-boat, when,
fortunately, we saw a small merchant-ship's boat
rowed by two naval seamen and called them alongside. They said they had just landed two officers
and were returning to their ship. They were just
as unconcerned as if they had been coming off from
a routine trip after dinner in peace time, although
bullets were coming over our lines and dropping all
around them. We got into their boat and after
several attempts and getting very wet, we got on
shore. We found ourselves on the right of our position in what was afterwards known as Anzac Cove.
Rows of wounded men were laid out in front of us
under the shelter of some rising ground. The doctors in charge, who evidently expected that the
beach might be rushed at any moment, implored me
to have them taken off as it was murder to leave
them there. I promised to do my best for them and
went off to find Birdwood who, I was told, was on
the beach, a little further along. The beach was
crowded with men ; some, exhausted after the strenuous day, had just thrown themselves down and
slept like logs ; some were getting food and drink
for the first time for many hours, others were being
collected by officers and N.C.O.'s and being formed
into organized units, being sent either to reinforce
the fighting line or to prepare positions to fall back
on in case of necessity. I found General Birdwood

sitting down with his Divisional Generals and Staff.
Birdwood, whom nothing could daunt and who is
never so happy as when in the fighting line, and for
preference in a tight place, was cheerful but not
very hopeful. I gave him Sir Ian's letter and said
I hoped he would be able to hold out till the morning
when we could take stock of the situation, and I
thought when daylight came, many of the isolated
positions we had seen holding on before dark, would
be able to join hands and form a continuous line on
which they could consolidate and dig themselves in.
After staying with him a short time, during which
we arranged the order in which further troops and
guns were to be landed, I returned to my ship,
arriving there soon after 4 a.m., just as dawn was
breaking. The wind and sea had gone down and
soon the sun rose and it turned into a glorious day.
Our men's spirits rose, the isolated positions got into
touch with each other and a line was established on
which they dug themselves in and were soon in a
very strong position, half a mile or so from the beach.

" In the meantime, troops, guns and stores were
being landed under incessant gun and rifle fire which
it was impossible for the covering ships to subdue
completely owing to the skilful manner in which
the enemy's guns were concealed, and occasional
bursts of fire from the enemy's ships in the Narrows
delayed the landing as the transports had to draw
out of range until our battleships had driven them
off.

" All the morning the enemy, now heavily reinforced, repeatedly attacked our line, but our men, full
of confidence, beat them off with great loss. They
had been fighting continuously since dawn on the

25th, and were getting very tired, but our position being now more or less secure, General Birdwood was able to relieve the men in the front line and commenced to reorganize his force and consolidate his position behind the fighting line. Afloat, hospital carriers had been fitted out, the wounded had been collected from the various ships in which they had been temporarily placed, and put on board them. The necessary medical officers and stores had not yet arrived, so the personnel of the Base Hospitals were distributed amongst them. There were only enough to provide two doctors to each hospital carrier, and as each of them carried from 600 to 800 wounded, some of them very severe cases, it is obvious they could not have received much attention until their arrival at Alexandria. It is very greatly to the credit of the medical officers on shore that I did not hear of a single case being sent on board that had not received efficient first aid and a first dressing on their wounds.

" Our position was now thoroughly established, the force reorganized, brigades, regiments, and companies had been sorted out and reformed, stores and ammunition accumulated behind the line and all was in readiness for a further advance. Our position on shore was somewhat as follows :—The right of our line rested on the beach on the high ground about a mile from Gaba Tepe, from there it ran inland on rough, hilly ground to an eminence about half a mile from the beach, overlooking the low undulating ground towards Kilid Bahr, thence irregularly in a northerly direction on hilly ground inundated with gullies and dry watercourses and covered with bushes and scrub as far as the high ground overlooking Fisherman's Hut for about 3,000 yards, and from there to the beach again.

" On each flank, close in, a destroyer was stationed with searchlights at night turned on to the shore to prevent a surprise attack on the beach. Further out, the *Bacchante* was anchored off Gaba Tepe, the *Majestic* and *Triumph* on each flank, while the *Queen, London,* and *Prince of Wales* were anchored in front of Anzac Beach with transports, store and supply ships anchored outside them.

" The fire of the enemy's ships in the Straits was so accurate that I suspected the presence of spotters either on Cape Nebrunesi on our left flank or on Gaba Tepe on our right flank. I sent the destroyer *Harpy* to examine Cape Nebrunesi at daylight (on the 27th). She landed a party and discovered a cut telegraph wire. Again on May 2 the *Colne* and *Usk* embarked a party of fifty men of the New Zealand Division who landed on Cape Nebrunesi at dawn where they surprised a Turkish patrol asleep in their trenches, three of whom were killed and the remainder made prisoners.

" It was not until May 4 that any troops could be spared to attack Gaba Tepe. I estimated that about 1,000 men would be required, 500 to advance along the beach and 500 to be landed from destroyers. The military authorities, however, decided that 120 would be sufficient, and asked me to arrange to land them from the sea. That number were accordingly embarked on board the destroyers *Colne, Chelmer* and *Usk,* the whole under the command of Commander C. Seymour of the *Usk.* The operation was timed to commence at dawn. The Peninsula having been thoroughly bombarded by the *Bacchante, Dart-*

mouth and *Ribble*, the men were landed but could make no headway. They got as far as a small ledge a few feet high about 15 or 20 yards from the water's edge and lay down under it, but although well supported by the fire of six ships, could not get any further. After remaining in this position for about an hour, and seeing no prospect of a further advance, they were withdrawn and re-embarked with the loss of three or four of their number who were left lying on the beach, presumably dead. As, however, one of them now and again made spasmodic movements, it was thought he might be alive, so a volunteer party was organized to go on shore and bring him off. A steam-boat over which floated a large red-cross flag towed a dinghy ashore with three men in it who jumped ashore and brought off the wounded man without being molested. As soon as they were well on their way to the ship, a party of Turkish soldiers was seen advancing towards the beach. On arriving there they faced the ship, presented arms and then grounded arms and proceeded to bury the dead. Having completed this task, they again fell in, presented arms and marched away. This little incident gave our men a high opinion of the chivalry of the Turkish soldier.

"On May 2, our forces having been thoroughly rested and reorganized and reinforced by some of the Naval Division, a further advance was decided on. This was very necessary since the left of our line of trenches ran along the top of some high cliffs and our men had to get into them by means of rope ladders and, if the trenches were stormed, they would have no means of retreat. We still had hopes of being able to capture Hill 971 which we looked upon

7

as the key to the whole position on the Peninsula. If we could once establish ourselves on it not only could we attack the enemy's communications, but we could also direct the fire of our ships at Anzac on the enemy's forts and positions in the Straits. A programme of firing in which every ship took part thoroughly searched the ground over which the advance was to take place. It was so intense that it seemed impossible for any living thing to have survived it. After half an hour's bombardment, fire ceased and the troops advanced. The operation, however, was only a partial success, 500 or 600 yards were gained. which relieved the situation in the trenches, but did not bring us much nearer to the coveted summit of the hill, and although we inflicted considerable loss on the enemy, we ourselves had over 700 casualties.

"Regular trench warfare was now commenced, reliefs organized, supplies arranged for. The area behind the fighting line was cleared, shell proof shelters were made for troops not in the firing line, for horses, mules and supplies of food and ammunition. There were a good many casualties behind the firing line from snipers concealed in the bushes and ravines. The task of clearing them out was entrusted to a small body of Ceylon planters who had volunteered for service and been attached to the Australian Division. They very soon made short work of any snipers remaining behind the lines; their methods were somewhat rough and ready but they were effectual.

"On May 6 the ships had to move out and anchor further from the beach to keep clear of the shrapnel shell from the enemy's guns and from the bullets from his trenches which came over our lines and fell on board and all around our ships causing some casualties. One of them killed a carpenter who was working on the stern walk outside my cabin.

"The fire of the Turkish ships in the Narrows was also becoming more accurate, several ships were hit, but no material damage done although there were many narrow shaves. One stands out in my memory. A destroyer was lying about 50 yards away from H.M.S. *Queen*, when a shell, probably an 11-inch one from the *Goeben*, fell between us. The destroyer was completely lost to view behind the huge volume of the splash. We all thought she had been hit and done for, but much to our relief, when the spray cleared away, she was seen to be still there, untouched, and her men laughing and cheering at their narrow escape.

"Another narrow escape may well be told here that occurred as the force was being landed. The coxswain of one of the destroyers who was steering his vessel was shot through both cheeks. The bullet passing through both cheeks took out two teeth on each side of his mouth and then killed a signalman who was standing alongside."

The Admiral proceeds to describe the transfer of an Australian Division to Helles and comments on the death of General Bridges, "who commanded the Australian Division. He was a most able and efficient officer and had the confidence and esteem of all who had anything to do with him. A sniper's bullet severed the arteries in his thigh, and although he was taken to a hospital ship, he died before he could reach Alexandria.

"General Birdwood himself had a very narrow

escape. He was, as usual, in the hottest part of the fighting line when he was struck by a bullet which grazed his scalp, cutting away the hair in its passage and making a regular parting on the top of his head. He was knocked down, but after a day in bed, was able to resume duty. It afterwards gave him considerable pain and trouble as it developed blood poisoning, but in spite of this he stuck to his work until after the final evacuation when he was able to lay up and have it properly treated."

Admiral Thursby, after having conducted his part of the operations in so brilliant a manner, turned over his duties as Senior Naval Officer off Anzac, on May 18, to Captain Grant of H.M.S. *Canopus* and sailed with part of his squadron to take command of the British Naval Forces that were to co-operate with the Italian Fleet in the Adriatic.

Early on the 25th the fleet of transports and supply ships had arrived from Mudros and anchored in our rear out of range of the enemy's guns. From the moment that W and X Beaches were in our possession a stream of tugs and steamboats towing lighters, barges and pontoons, laden with guns, ammunition and stores commenced to flow to and fro from the ships to the beaches, a stream which never ceased for more than three weeks and was only eventually brought to an end when the menace of submarines drove this fleet into the shelter of Mudros harbour.

Since the *Euryalus* was, for the time being, General Hunter Weston's Headquarters, her movements were to a great extent governed by his requirements and we passed from one beach to another as necessity dictated, constantly firing at such targets as the enemy from time to time presented. As many of the wounded as possible were brought on board to give relief to the hospital ships and amongst others Brig.-General Hare, who was placed in my cabin. During the afternoon I snatched a minute to go down and see how he was getting on and to my consternation discovered the cabin empty with only a few traces of blood, nobody had found time to remove, to show that he had been there. Nobody knew anything about him and I was much concerned at his disparition and wondered whether he were still alive. It was only much later that I learned, greatly to my relief, that he had been taken off to a hospital ship without the knowledge of any of my people.

"April 27. . . . Sunday, April 25, was a marvellous day. When last I wrote we were steaming over to Tenedos where the last phase of the preparations took place. On the 24th the 3,000 troops that formed the advance party were removed from their transports to the *Euryalus*, *Cornwallis* and *Implacable* and the ninety odd boats in which they were landed for the attack had to be prepared. In the morning it was blowing fresh and it looked as though at the very last moment we should again have to postpone the attack. I spent some very miserable hours, for I had to make up my mind by 2 p.m. whether the last preparations should proceed and at 1.30 there seemed but little appearance of the wind going down. At ten minutes to two, however, there was a change for the better and so the work was commenced and all went smoothly. We left Tenedos at 10 p.m. the *Euryalus*, *Cornwallis* and *Implacable* with some trawlers having between us ninety open boats in tow and steamed slowly in a perfectly smooth sea towards Helles. At 4 a.m., still pitch dark, we stopped and the troops were transferred to the boats. Nothing went wrong, not the smallest detail had been forgotten and when one comes to analyze what this means, one cannot help feeling proud and thankful—so small a mistake might have spelt so huge a disaster. And so, at the appointed time (ten minutes late to be accurate) they started off, and to see them as the day was dawning going in towards the beaches, which we knew to be so strongly protected, as regularly as it were a parade, was a sight I can never forget. The beaches had already been heavily bombarded by the Fleet in the hopes of destroying the wire entanglements by which they were protected, but as the boats approached the firing ceased. Try to imagine my feelings, as I was standing on the bridge, by the side of Hunter Weston, watching them, knowing that so far as I was concerned I could do nothing more to help them except to open fire on an unseen enemy in well-concealed trenches on the cliffs above, which one did with a will. Imagine, if you can, the positive sickness that came over one when one saw the leading men jump out of the boats only to be shot down as they got mixed up in the wire entanglements, a feeling of sickness which changed gradually to one of exulting pride as it dawned upon one that nothing was going to stop them. The seamen were just as magnificent. One saw boats manned by wounded men, struggling back to the ships, to get more troops, never for one instant hesitating, these men without means of firing back on the enemy, with only oars in their hands. I am not sure that I do not think that theirs was the higher courage if there could be any differentiating. By two o'clock in the afternoon we had landed 13,000 men, an hour earlier than I had anticipated. At one spot an old collier, the *River Clyde* suitably fitted to carry 2,000 men, had been run on shore, and it was hoped that her troops could be rapidly and immediately disembarked straight from the ship. This, however, was not to be, for owing to the heavy fire to which she was subjected, the lighters she was towing and which were to be the bridge by which the troops were to be landed got adrift and could not be got into their position. The ship was magnificently handled by Unwin, who has since earned the V.C. several times over. He with two midshipmen and two seamen performed perfect prodigies of valour and heroism, both in trying to connect the lighters and in saving life. These men seemed to bear charmed lives, for though all around them were being shot down like rabbits, they escaped with a few grazes from bullets which did them no harm. One seaman was eventually killed, but the others all escaped and are all well and hard at work. By 9 a.m. we actually had a fairly secure footing on the Peninsula.

" Now—two days afterwards—I can hardly believe it, and I now realize that I never really believed that we should succeed ! but I would not allow myself to believe that anything but success was possible. But I now know that had I allowed myself to think too much, I should have thought failure a certainty. So far as I was concerned I was determined to avert disaster and in that way everybody was alike, thank God, with the result that the apparently impossible has been accomplished.

" Look at the maps and then try and realize that we landed 6,000 men on two small beaches at the end of the Peninsula in a few minutes under heavy fire, on beaches that were a mass of barbed wire entanglements and covered from every quarter by Maxims and well-concealed rifle pits. The Lancashire Fusiliers covered themselves with glory, and so did the bluejackets who pulled them ashore in the boats. At one of the beaches the first lot to attempt landing were practically annihilated before they reached the shore and sinking boats containing nothing but dead drifting about was the result. It was here that the *River Clyde* was beached and indeed she proved a refuge for the bulk of the troops in her who remained in her comparatively secure until darkness made it possible for them to land. Had it not been for her I do not think it is an exaggeration to say we should not now be where we are. . . ."

CHAPTER V

THERE had been some rain in the course of the night. Occasional outbursts of musketry during the dark hours had told of counter attacks, but the morning of the 26th broke clear on a situation seemingly unchanged. But only seemingly. Immediately darkness had set in Commander Unwin had re-established the bridge between the *River Clyde* and the shore, and the imprisoned troops after a day of untold trial had quietly crept out of the ship and been joined by the few survivors of the morning's attack who had ever since been sheltering in dug-outs under the sand-ridges. Those on the left had established communication with the Worcestershires on Cape Helles and entrenched themselves close to the ruins of Fort No. 1, whilst those on the right had found shelter under the walls of Fort Sedd-el-Bahr. At daylight the latter tried to work round into the village, but were prevented from so doing by the fire of a machine gun in the fort. This however was quickly disposed of by the *Albion*, who, in response to a signal from the *River Clyde*, turned her guns on to the remaining tower, which after a few rounds collapsed. Colonel Doughty Wylie eventually brought this party through the village, and after an intense bombardment of the slopes by ships' guns stormed the old castle, which was gained by ten o'clock. After a pause here and under cover of further fire from the ships

107

he led his men to the final attack on the redoubt of
Hill 141, the last position dominating the beach,
and as he entered it at the head of the troops he
fell dead—shot in the head.   It was a splendid feat
of arms carried out by the troops who for more
than twenty-four hours had suffered almost every
torment that war can inflict, led by a gallant officer
and a great gentleman who died at the moment
of a success due solely to his initiative and not inferior
to any in history. The retreating Turks were
severely punished by the *Lord Nelson*, who from
her position off Morto Bay was able to shell them
as they fled. At last, after unheard-of sacrifices
and through unsurpassed gallantry, W Beach was
open to us and our line was established from Tekke
Burnu to Sedd-el-Bahr.

At about 7 a.m. a signal from the *Queen Elizabeth*
had informed General Hunter Weston that a French
Brigade was available, and this the General, unaware
of what was happening at Sedd-el-Bahr, proposed
to put on shore at W Beach for the purpose of
capturing Hill 141 and the Redoubt from Cape Helles.
The French transports were therefore ordered up,
but before the disembarkation could begin, Colonel
Doughty Wylie's brilliant feat had altered the whole
aspect of the situation and the French contingent
were enabled to land at V Beach, where the *River
Clyde*, under the indefatigable Commander Unwin,
was being converted into a pier.

As a set-off to this success came the news of the,
to us, inexplicable retirement from Y Beach. It
will be remembered that the landing here had been
unopposed, and that Sir Ian Hamilton's proposal of
the day before that the troops that had been unable

to land on V Beach should be diverted to Y Beach, had been rejected by General Hunter Weston, as causing too much delay. The enemy had left the force at Y severely alone during the daytime, but all through the night, when he had nothing to fear from the ships' guns, our men had been subjected to continual attacks by superior forces which, though successfully repulsed, had left them in a weak and critical state. At daylight when, as was thought, the enemy was dispersed by ships' fire, the worn-out party began to carry the wounded down to the beach and asked for ships' boats to embark them. Colonel Matthews, who was in command, sent a message to General Hunter Weston saying he could not hold his position without fresh ammunition and reinforcements. This message never reached its destination. Whether the men mistook the order for evacuating the wounded as one for evacuating the beach is unknown, but they did begin to leave the trenches, when the enemy promptly attacked them once more, but once more was beaten off. The ships, believing that evacuation had been ordered, were doing their utmost to further what they concluded to be the General's order and sent every available boat to the beaches and the *Sapphire* asked the *Queen Elizabeth*, approaching from Gaba Tepe, to open fire on the ridge to cover the re-embarkation. This the *Queen Elizabeth* did for some little time, and Sir Ian Hamilton, not understanding the reason for this movement, but believing that the order for evacuation had been given by General Hunter Weston, came on to us to have the matter elucidated. Until this moment we on board the *Euryalus* had been in blissful ignorance of what

was occurring at Y, and Sir Ian Hamilton's surprise
at learning that no orders for such a move had been
given was no greater than was ours at hearing what
had taken place.

The French forces having been successfully withdrawn from Kum-Kale during the night of the 26th
–27th were in their transports off Tenedos ready
to disembark where and when required. Their first
brigade, landed on V Beach on the 26th, were moved
straight up and took over the right of the line and
the men-of-war took up positions in readiness to
support the advance which it was proposed to make
early on the 27th ; but in order to give the tired
troops as much rest as possible, the attack was
postponed till 4 p.m. At noon, however, the enemy
delivered an attack from Krithia that was easily
repulsed with the ships' assistance, and when we
pushed on we did so without encountering resistance
and the worn-out force dug itself in on a line running
from Gully Beach to De Tott's Battery, hoping to
get the essential repose before attacking on the
following day.

There seems to have been no reason why, had
our men not been prevented by fatigue, we should
not have gone straight on and captured Achi-Baba ;
but after three days and two nights of hard fighting,
of digging and of carrying ammunition, supplies
and water, with losses calculated at little short of
50 per cent., the troops were brought to a standstill by sheer exhaustion. The nearest reinforcements were still on the high seas between Egypt and
Mudros—of reserves there were none. Those who
have read Sir Ian Hamilton's Gallipoli *Diary* will
realize how the policy of starvation in this matter

crippled us from the very outset, for who can doubt that had the usual reserves been now available, Achi-Baba, the key of the situation, the object of our attack, would this day have been ours and the issue of the campaign been no longer in doubt.

The 2-mile advance had the effect of somewhat easing the congestion on the beaches that up till now had ever been growing greater as more guns, ammunition, mules and all the paraphernalia of a modern army were landed. The beach parties of naval ratings under Captain Phillimore, of the wounded *Inflexible*, had been hard at work night and day, clearing lighters, building piers, carrying ammunition to the fighting line and helping with the wounded. Theirs was a task of hard manual labour carried out with the proverbial cheerfulness of the British bluejacket, who is apt to regard any work performed outside his own ship, whatever its nature, in the light of a picnic. On this occasion there was an extra spur to exertion, if indeed that were needed, in their admiration for the gallantry of their comrades of the Sister Service who for so many hours had been fighting, fighting, fighting. Without arms they could not follow their hearts into the trenches, but they could, and did, assist by supplying ammunition and helping to evacuate the wounded.

At Gaba Tepe the morning of the 27th had been heralded in by a severe shelling of the beach on the part of the enemy, causing some damage and considerable delay in the work of disembarkation. An aeroplane reported that the *Goeben* was just above the Narrows and that the shelling was coming from her. With the *Manica's* kite-balloon the *Queen*

Elizabeth prepared to engage her across the Peninsula and opened fire at 9 a.m. That was the end
of the shelling as far as the *Goeben* was concerned,
for although not hit, she shifted her position close
in, under the cliffs, from whence her projectiles
could not reach the Australian beach. Shortly
afterwards two enemy transports were reported in
the same position that the *Goeben* had just vacated,
and once more the *Queen Elizabeth* tried what she
could do, with the aid of a balloon to spot for her.
Her second shot hit one of the transports which sank
immediately.

Quite apart from the direct result of this astonish-
ing feat of gunnery, it was hoped that this incident
would have considerable moral effect on the enemy
and help to upset his arrangements for reinforcing
the Peninsula by sea. But these were not the only
means which Admiral de Robeck counted upon to
achieve this end. Two French submarines had
attempted to get through the Straits, but both had
failed. One, the *Bernouli*, unable to stem the current
at the Narrows, had been swept out again, whilst
the other, the *Joula*, had the misfortune to be destroyed by a mine. The Australian Submarine
A.E. 2 (Lieut.-Commander H. Stoker) had better
success, and getting into the Marmora without
incident, tried to attack two battleships above the
Narrows, attempts frustrated by the smoothness of
the sea ; but three days afterwards she was sunk
by a Turkish torpedo boat, who saved all her crew
and made them prisoners.

On the following morning, the 28th, the attack
was opened with a preparatory bombardment by
the Fleet, the *Lord Nelson, Vengeance, Cornwallis*

and *Albion* being stationed on the right, the *Implacable*, *Goliath*, *Dublin* and *Sapphire* on the left, with the *Euryalus* and *Swiftsure* off W Beach, whilst the *Queen Elizabeth*, with Sir Ian Hamilton still on board, moved about as necessity dictated. The rising sun behind the land was always a hindrance to good shooting in the morning, and on this occasion the conditions were rendered even worse by a mist lying on the shore so that the firing could at the best be but blind.

The advance commenced just before 10 a.m. and at first encountered no resistance. Our left flank had reached Y Beach when the *Queen Elizabeth*, who was following up, observed a strong company of Turks on the top of the cliffs about to attack the old trenches in which were now our men. The enemy's first rush brought him to a position enfiladed by her guns, and with one shrapnel that burst just in front of it she annihilated the whole company, computed at not less than 100 men. In spite of this powerful assistance, the left was brought to a standstill by cleverly concealed machine guns, impossible to locate from the sea; and the centre, which by noon had reached a position within a mile of Krithia, could not push forward on account of the check to the left. The French on the right were also held up, and all along the line a shortage of ammunition, due to the difficulties in getting it from the congested beaches, was making itself felt. Some of the Royal Naval Division, who had been pushed up into the firing line, were now therefore withdrawn to act as supply parties, and their returning to the beaches led a number of officerless troops around them to believe that a general retirement

had been ordered. They were nevertheless quickly
rallied and the mistake rectified, but the incident
gave the enemy a chance of counter-attacking he
was not slow to avail himself of. The counter-
attack was repulsed, but left our still imperfectly
rested troops too exhausted to do anything more
and by sunset they were dug in on a line between
De Tott's and Y Beach. The enemy had also
suffered severely and was in no condition to renew
the fighting, and the next two days were spent in
re-organizing and resting the worn-out troops.

"April 28, 1915. . . . The battle still continues,
our people are advancing but slowly. They are
awfully tired, but every moment we are putting
ashore more men, more guns and more ammunition
and I sincerely hope that more of each are on their
way out from England, for I know we shall require
them. Our losses are very heavy, nearly 50 per
cent., I fear. . . . I cannot help rejoicing that
I have had something to do with this extraordinary
achievement, as after all the old *Euryalus*, with
Burmester, Marriott, Bevan and myself in her, led
the attack. . . ."

The evening of the 28th did not lessen our difficulties nor allay our anxieties, for it came on to
blow sufficiently hard to render the landing of our
stores on the exposed beaches and unprotected piers
impossible. The abandonment of the work of disembarkation awoke gloomy forebodings as to the
results of two or three days of bad weather. Such
an eventuality was improbable at this time of year,
but even the remote possibility of the Army being
imprisoned on the Peninsula with but little ammunition and no reserves of rations caused me grave

preoccupation, for so slender was our margin in this respect that at that time we had not more than one day's rations on shore. But the breeze did not last many hours and work was again in full swing on the following morning.

Although there was a temporary lull in the fighting on shore, the Navy never ceased to be actively employed. The Asiatic batteries that since the evacuation of Kum-Kale had been giving much trouble, particularly at V Beach where the *River Clyde* seemed to be their favourite target, were constantly being engaged by our ships who did not escape scatheless. The *Agamemnon* and the *Henri IV* received a good deal of damage, though not happily of a serious nature, whilst the *Albion* was sufficiently severely wounded as to necessitate her return to Mudros for repairs. The *Wolverine* had the misfortune to lose her Captain, Commander Prentis, killed by a shell bursting on the fore bridge, and hardly a ship engaged without sustaining some casualty. Moreover a considerable number of men were absent from their ships, serving in beach parties or on board transports, tugs, and boats, so that the strain at this time was severe, and all the more so since the majority of the crews were reservists, splendid men but on whom the stress told more heavily than on younger ones.

A conspicuous feature of the operations during those first strenuous and fateful days was the conduct of the midshipmen. The majority had, on the outbreak of war, been sent to sea before completing their full period of training at Dartmouth and were, in truth, little more than children. In spite of their youth and inexperience they handled the men and

8

boats committed to their charge with a firmness, courage, and determination that was truly admirable. On April 24 they were boys of whom one felt one should not expect too much ; three days later they had developed into young men on whose ability to carry out their duties with success one could place complete reliance, and without exception they proved themselves capable of dealing with difficult situations that spoke volumes for their character and for their training.

With the object of looking for further places for disembarkation which would relieve the growing congestion on the beaches, I landed for the first time on April 30, and in company with General Hunter Weston examined the coast, but without success. Our search afforded me an opportunity of examining the enemies' cleverly constructed trenches, and I marvelled at the gallantry of the troops that had effected a landing against them.

The scene presented by the beaches was unparalleled, presenting as it did activity in its most intense form. At one and the same time piers were under construction, roads being made, dug-outs excavated, stores and ammunition landed and stowed away in such small space as might be considered clear of shell-fire, whilst horses and mules were being coaxed or shoved from the water's edge to the shelter of the cliffs. Looking down upon this teeming hive from the cliffs above produced the impression of perpetual motion, for nothing in the crowded space was ever still for one moment, except that line of stretchers bearing wounded men awaiting their turn of embarkation.

" May 1st. . . . There has been no fighting for

the last two days, both sides exhausted. . . . We have a pretty firm footing on the Peninsula now, and it does not seem likely that the enemy will be able to turn us out. I do not think that the people in England can possibly grasp the magnitude of the job that we have undertaken. I do not think they can grasp that the almost impossible has been achieved. An order of Liman von Sanders was found on the body of a dead German officer to-day in which he said that the Peninsula had been made impregnable and that no troops could ever effect a landing on it.

"Truly the British Tommy and bluejacket are marvellous creatures. I have visited the trenches —they are wonderfully cleverly constructed, which only makes one wonder all the more at the gallantry of our men. . . . It is a long, long way to Constantinople, and it can only be shortened by the collapse of the Turk, and although I hope for this and refuse to think it impossible, I do not believe it likely until the Fleet can get through the Straits and now that cannot be until we have the Peninsula in our hands."

Soon after ten o'clock on the evening of May 1, I had just finished writing and was thinking of going to bed, when suddenly the perfect stillness pervading until that moment was broken by a sudden roar of artillery. It was an attack by the enemy! We on board could do nothing, for there were no means by which the ships could give the troops any assistance. It was not long before the rattle of musketry and shouts and hurrahs reached us across the water, proclaiming that the combatants were coming to close quarters. All night long stories reached us of the ebb and flow of the battle, and at one time there were ugly rumours of our line being pierced and of a possible retreat to the beaches. It was not until the early morning that we learnt what had happened. It appeared that there had been some critical moments in which the enemy had actually pierced our lines, but the mistake had been quickly rectified and the enemy repulsed, and just before daylight a counter-attack on our part was ordered. In spite of their exhaustion, our troops advanced with great spirit and were only checked by concealed machine guns that they were unable to rush owing to their physical exhaustion. They were obliged to return to their trenches, but daylight enabled the ships to open fire on the retreating enemy, whose losses were very heavy. We also had suffered severely, and though the enemy's attack had failed, and we were safely entrenched in the original lines, our counter-attack had been checked and we were no nearer attaining Achi-Baba than before.

The evidences of the night's hard fighting were distressingly visible in the large numbers of wounded that came pouring back from the fighting line. There was neither place nor appliances for dealing with these poor fellows on shore, and the shortage of boats caused much delay in getting them afloat. The hospital ships were already full to overflowing and had been sent off to Alexandria to land their pathetic cargoes, and the only thing that could be done was to accommodate as many as possible in such ships as could be found for them. Empty transports were made use of, but though they gave shelter, they had neither doctors nor medical stores. The men-o'-war took in as many as they could, but still the numbers increased, and I heartily cursed the lack of foresight that had allowed such an expedition to be undertaken with means so inadequate.

Later in the evening of the 2nd, the *Albion*, operating on the right flank, was again hit by a shell from the Asiatic shore and sustained damage severe enough to render her return to Mudros for repairs necessary.

The night witnessed another heavy attack on the part of the enemy, the brunt of which was borne by the French on the right. It was repulsed with heavy losses, but renewed again on the following night with the same results.

During the morning of the 3rd, I was with General d'Amade in the trenches, watching an endeavour on the part of the French to improve their position. From where I stood a wonderful view was obtained; in front the plain gradually sloping towards Achi-Baba; on the right, Morto Bay and the entrance of the Straits, where the *Prince George* was stationed on the enemy's left. I was watching the advance of the Senegalese troops, and as my glasses, moving from left to right, reached the end of their line, the *Prince George* came into the field of vision. At that very moment she was hit by a 6-inch shell coming from the Asiatic shore. She took a slight list and moved her position, and though for some time she continued the support that she was giving, subsequent examination showed that her wound was sufficiently serious to necessitate her return to Malta for repairs. To see a battleship hit and troops advancing at one and the same time is an unusual experience.

If the Army was exhausted by incessant fighting the Navy also was feeling the strain. Owing to so many men having been withdrawn for work in the transports, in boats, and on the beaches, the drain on the personnel was great, and this state of affairs having existed for more than a week, steps had to be taken to relieve them.

Before leaving Mudros, I had started the enrolment of a Greek Labour Corps, which by now had reached considerable dimensions, and was sufficiently well organized to permit of their being sent to the transports to take the place of the bluejackets. Since the work required of them was being performed beyond the reach of the enemy's guns, there was no difficulty in getting the Greeks to carry it out, and the bluejackets thus relieved became available for other duties. By this means the strain was somewhat eased, enabling some much-needed relief to be given to the beach parties.

"May 5. . . . I wish I could give you some idea of the sight that meets the eye from the deck of this ship. In front that wonderfully inhospitable shore, gradually rising to the great peak called Achi-Baba, the goal for which we are striving, the key to the situation, which it is hoped to capture to-morrow. On the beach thousands of men making roads and piers, unloading lighters of their freights of guns, ammunition, stores, etc., the low cliffs crowned by masses of horses, mules, men, tents, hospitals—all crowded because they have to be out of the range of possible shell-fire. On the right the entrance to the Dardanelles with the magnificent Asiatic mountains in the distance. To the right and left, battleships and cruisers which occasionally open fire on points indicated from aeroplanes by wireless telegraphy. Behind us, clusters of transports, ships of all descriptions, from huge liners to the ordinary collier, and the whole surface of the sea dotted with steamboats of all descriptions, towing laden lighters to the beach and empty ones back—one has only to land and walk for a few minutes to find oneself in a position from which one can see the enemy's lines. From here one gets a gorgeous view over the Plain which gradually rises to and ends in the aforesaid Achi-Baba.

" To-day I have been busy writing despatches— one of them recommending those four fine fellows (Commander Unwin, Midshipmen Drewry and Malleson, and Seaman Samson) for the V.C. It is a great pleasure doing so, but it is difficult to find suitable language without being gushing.

" I look back at the last ten days and wonder how on earth we have got through with so little assistance from home. We are handling nearly twice as many transports as they have every day at any one time at Southampton, without any proper transport officers. We have landed an Army of nearly 100,000 men with only the resources of the Fleet, and such additional boats, lighters, etc., as they could get hold of locally, and all the time the ships have been actively engaged in supporting the Army. It has been a very wonderful piece of work, and the greatest praise is due to the officers and men for the magnificent way in which they have fought and worked. We have gone through an experience which I should think no one will ever have again, and if we are eventually successful, it will not be due to any help or encouragement that we have received from the

Admiralty. I have always said, and always will say, that the Admiralty is much too well served. The Navy and the Army have worked well together and there has not been the slightest friction, and this I think is rather wonderful considering the absolutely different point of view from which each service looks upon things in general.

" The transportation of the wounded from the fighting line to the hospital ships has not been an easy matter, especially at the beginning, but it goes rather better now. And those wounded! Truly they are heroes. Never a word of complaint whatever their sufferings or discomforts. One is indeed proud of one's countrymen."

" May 7. . . . The advance continues, but slowly. The difficulties are very great and have I fear been much under-estimated. The soldiers are wonderfully optimistic and I hope we may win through in the end, but it will cost us more than they expected. I believe that the Authorities at home thought that, once we were landed, the business would be over. Our difficulties have not been lessened the last two days by a fresh breeze which does not facilitate a landing of stores. However, everybody works with a will, and consequently the difficulties are reduced to a minimum."

In the meantime the situation of the Australians at Gaba Tepe had been considerably improved and there seemed but little chance of the enemy being now able to dislodge them from the position they had so hardly and gallantly won. Sir Ian Hamilton therefore decided to take advantage of this security to reinforce the troops in the Southern Area by two brigades of General Birdwood's men for a further attack being planned for May 6. These 6,000 men were moved round to Helles on the night of the 5th–6th in destroyers and fleet-sweepers, but the operation was much hampered by bad weather, causing considerable difficulty and delay in embarking them. In spite of these adverse circumstances, however, the two brigades were got away by 4 a.m. on the 6th and landed at Helles without further interruption. The attack was opened by the usual bombardment on the part of the Fleet, now reduced by two units, the *Albion* and *Prince George*, both temporarily out of action, from wounds received a few days before. The intensity of the fire had perforce to be of a somewhat restricted nature, owing to the shortage of ammunition which was beginning to be felt. The advance commenced at 11.30 and encountered strong resistance, but progress was made all along the line, except on the extreme left, where a hidden redoubt, close to Y Beach, proved an insurmountable object. The fighting ceased at 4.30 and our troops dug themselves in on a new line preparatory to renewing the attack on the following day. No success, however, could be expected whilst this formidable redoubt remained in existence to frustrate the advance on the left, and an attempt to deal with it was made the next morning by the *Swiftsure* and *Talbot* with the help of a kite balloon. All efforts on the part of the latter to locate it failed, and in spite of the *Swiftsure* closing in and subjecting the area to an intense bombardment, no results were achieved, for the configuration of the land prevented her projectiles from reaching the redoubt—situated as it was, on ground sloping away inland from the edge of the cliff and therefore inaccessible to direct fire. The fighting on this day (the 7th) followed closely on the lines of that of the day before, with the same result of a slight advance in the centre and on the right, where the enemy was driven back almost into the village of Krithia, but of a check on the left, and once more did the troops dig themselves in for the night. On the following morning (the 8th) the *Queen Elizabeth* with the kite balloon made another attempt to reduce the redoubt, but the balloon was no more successful in locating it on this occasion than she had been before.

The New Zealanders who were now on the left of the line attempted to advance against it, but could make no progress. Sir Ian Hamilton, realizing that exhausted nature would not permit of much more fighting, ordered a general advance to take place at 5.30 p.m. after a quarter of an hour's general bombardment. At 5.15, in spite of the anxiety caused by the growing shortage of ammunition, every gun, naval or land, that could be brought to bear, burst forth into a roar, which ceased at 5.30 as suddenly as it had commenced. Bayonets were fixed and the whole line charged. I watched the battle from a position close to General Hunter Weston's quarters, which gave me a view of nearly the whole line. Rays of the afternoon sun at my back struck the bayonets as they were fixed, producing the effect of a silver ribbon being drawn right across the Peninsula, but the continuity of this silver line was quickly dissolved into parties of men, surging backwards and forwards as the battle ebbed and flowed, until darkness hid them from view, when the battle ceased and the fighting died out from pure exhaustion. Though the fighting had temporarily ceased, it was recognized that, on its resumption, no progress could be made until the formidable redoubt close up to Y Beach was reduced and an attempt to capture it by surprise was planned.

A steep bluff to the northward of Y Beach gave this redoubt a natural protection from infantry attack on the flank, and, as has been said, the land sloping inward from the top of this bluff prevented it from being reached by the projectiles of the ships' guns. The bluff was sufficiently unclimbable to engender hopes that the enemy would consider any attempt to gain access to the higher land by its means impossible. This was the manner in which it was proposed to attempt its capture. A first attempt on the night of the 9th failed. The Gurkhas, to whom the enterprise was entrusted, after crawling down to Y Beach, crept along to its foot and scaled it, but directly they reached the top, they were detected and met with such heavy opposition that they were obliged to retire. The failure, however, was not to be taken as final, and on the night of the 12th the attempt was renewed. A joint naval and military reconnaissance from a destroyer during the daylight hours of the 11th, enabled plans to be drawn up for giving naval assistance. Directly after dark the Gurkhas began a repetition of their tactics of the 9th, but this time a brigade on the cliffs above, made a feint of a direct attack on the redoubt with artillery support, and as the Gurkhas passed the beach, two men-o'-war, the *Dublin* and *Talbot*, opened a heavy fire on the gulley. Reaching the foot of the bluff without opposition, the attackers succeeded in scaling the bluff and reached the top unperceived by the enemy, whose attention had been fully taken up by the feint attack. Immediately they reached the high ground they entrenched themselves in and were speedily reinforced, and in the morning Y Beach was once more in our possession and the position of the enemy in the redoubt untenable.

At the same time this daring and successful operation was being carried out, a catastrophe occurred on the opposite flank.

At about 1.30 a.m. on May 13 I had just turned in after a long evening's writing and was half asleep when I became aware of a certain amount of movement and evident excitement on deck. Whilst still in that half-conscious state which exists between properly awake and properly asleep, and consequently not quite sure whether the disturbance was not part of a dream, I was brought to a sudden sense of reality by my orderly opening the door and saying that he believed a ship had been sunk. In a second I had slipped on a great-coat and was on deck. The officer of the watch told me that something, the nature of which was not quite clear, had happened at the entrance of the Straits, hidden from our sight by Cape Helles, whose outline was lit up by the rays of searchlights beyond. All available boats from the ships had already been despatched to the scene and I could only remain with my glasses fixed on the point, awaiting evidence of what was happening. What had occurred was that the *Goliath*, the guard-ship at the mouth of the Straits, had been attacked by an enemy torpedo-boat. The torpedo got home and the ship sunk in a few minutes, leaving that portion of the crew that did not go down with her struggling in the water. The current, running swiftly out of the Straits, carried them with it, and as they were swept past the Cape, the searchlights ever playing on them to assist the boats in their work of rescue, there appeared to our horrified eyes a vision of men struggling in the water, all the clearer for the surrounding darkness. The night was perfectly still and it was difficult to believe that the fighting line lay only a few hundred yards away—and now this stillness was broken by an indistinct noise as of an angry crowd in the distance, a noise which gradually rose and fell and finally subsided, as the men were picked up or drowned—until at last stillness once more reigned and no signs were left of the tragedy that had so suddenly overtaken the *Goliath*—gone to the bottom before she came into our view.

Other anxieties and hard work helped quickly to overcome the feelings that this catastrophe evoked, but one could not help reflecting on the differences between naval and military warfare, which this event so vividly showed up. It has been computed that in shore fighting it takes several tons of lead to kill one man ; at sea one torpedo can cause the death of many hundreds. On shore the soldier is in almost perpetual discomfort, if not misery—at sea the sailor lives in comparative comfort until the moment comes when his life is required of him.

Destroyers were immediately despatched to try and cut off the retreat of the victorious torpedo-boat running back into the Narrows, triumphantly proclaiming by means of her wireless telegraphy that she had sunk an English battleship.

It was a maddening thought that she should escape scot free, but the patches of fog which had helped her in the successful attack, now enabled her to escape our pursuing destroyers.

During the afternoon of the 14th the enemy began to turn their attention towards some of the supply ships which, owing to the immunity they hitherto had had from these guns, had been brought closer to the beaches than was really safe, in order that the work of disembarking the stores might be hastened.

The store-ship *Ajax*, loaded with hay, was unfortunate enough to be hit by a shell, causing an outbreak of fire, which however was quickly got under. Her position of course was immediately shifted to a place of safety, and I visited her the next morning to see the damage that had been done, when her master showed me a curious instance of the effect of the flight of a projectile. The shell had passed right through his sleeping cabin and had pierced a bulkhead about 2 feet above a small shelf on which were some trifling objects, amongst them a half-crown piece. This coin, whilst still remaining on the shelf, had become twisted as though by the hands of some giant. He assured me that beyond a hole in the bulkhead this was the only evidence in the cabin of the flight of the projectile, nothing else had been disturbed.

CHAPTER VI

THOUGH the opening phases of the campaign had not resulted in the capture of the Kilid Bahr plain, the Army had succeeded in gaining a footing on the Peninsula from which it did not seem likely it could be driven. On the other hand voluntary withdrawal without disaster appeared equally impossible, and we were therefore committed to that very line of action that the Government so ardently had desired to avoid, for our dearly-bought experience proved that the objective could not be gained without a far greater expenditure of effort than our commitments in France could afford. Large reinforcements were necessary before any success could be hoped for, but owing to the lack of depth behind the fighting line precluding the establishment of camps on the Peninsula, it would be impossible to take them straight there and they would have to be brought to Mudros. Under these circumstances it was evident that the base would have to be expanded and developed, and I felt that my presence would be more necessary there than at Helles, where the arrangements for the disembarkation of troops and stores were working well. After consultation therefore with de Robeck I returned to Lemnos, hauled down my flag in the *Euryalus* and once more established myself on board the *Hussar*, whose cramped space now seemed more intolerable than ever.

Whilst hopes of an early success that would have

given us possession of the Peninsula were still entertained, it was comprehensible and perhaps even
natural that the military authorities should have
hesitated to expend money and energy on a base
which, under such circumstances, might have proved
unnecessary; but now that all such expectations had
perforce to be abandoned, it was disappointing to find
that they yet did not realize the necessity for its
development. In vain did I point out that piers
were essential, the establishment of camps and hospitals imperative; for more than a month nothing in
this direction was done.

Our Allies, however, had been more far-sighted and
were busy making those preparations for which I
pleaded in vain. The difficulty in getting anything
done was not lessened by the absence of any permanent military officer with authority requisite for
putting such works into execution. Personalities
were for ever changing; officers with whom I had
come to an arrangement one day disappeared the
next—perhaps to Egypt—perhaps to the front.

"Mudros, May 17, 1915. . . . The comparative
quiet of this place is refreshing, for during the last
three weeks there has scarcely been an hour of the
day or night when there has not been a booming of
guns or rattle of musketry. My work of landing the
Army over, I have returned here to develop the base
and there is much to be done. The requirements
are ever increasing, but the ways of meeting them
do not augment in proportion. The Admiralty
still pay but slight heed to our demands, and consequently it is the old story of bricks without straw.
The natives seem to have settled down quite amicably
under the new state of affairs, but they are untrust-

worthy devils. The transport business is becoming a very big affair indeed, and the wretched staff are under-manned and over-worked. . . .

"May 19. . . . We are in a curious position. Like Mahomet's coffin we seem to be suspended between two uncertainties. Whilst I am certain that this place must of necessity develop and become a huge base, the Admiralty on the contrary seem to think that nothing is required here, and that we ought to be able to carry out the work of a Portsmouth dockyard with no appliances and insufficient men. Last night was a regular gala in the matter of news. First of all, we were told that the Austrian army in the Bukovina is in disorderly flight, and then we hear that the resignations of Fisher and Winston Churchill are expected. We hear talk of a Coalition Cabinet. Of course that should have been formed at the beginning of the war. Evidently there are doings in the wind, but I fear it may be only a case of out of the frying-pan into the fire. Yesterday was the Czar's birthday and I had to go on board the *Askold*, the Russian cruiser here, to offer my congratulations. I was obliged to drink sweet champagne in the middle of the day, which I very much dislike. What an extraordinary nation they are! They seem quite undaunted by their many reverses and always come up smiling. I see by your letters that the reports given out in London about the landing must have been very vague. I suppose that, as usual, the authorities wanted to make matters out to be better than they really were. The truth is, that the getting on shore at all was a magnificent feat accompanied of course by tremendous losses. The army expected that, once on shore, they would be able to push on

9

quicker than has been the case, and therein lies the
disappointment. Things were under-estimated ; the
original fault of course was in attacking the forts
before the army was ready to be put on shore.

" May 20. . . . Two nights ago the Turks
delivered a great attack on the Australians, who
behaved splendidly and drove them off with great
slaughter. I hear nothing but good of them. I
have been so busy with matters naval lately, that I
have not had time to put my foot on shore to see for
myself how matters are going there. So many transports, supply ships, store ships, etc., and they all
require much looking after, and I am always suffering
from a shortage of everything. After the tension of
preparing for the landing and the excitement of those
first days at the Dardanelles everybody here is beginning to feel a little reaction. Luckily all my people
are good-tempered and work famously, but it is all
collar-work, and people at home do not help. I
could do with hundreds more officers and men and
material of all sorts. I suppose they havè difficulty
in finding them at home, but that does not make
matters any the easier for us. . . .

" Feeling in Greece against the Queen is beginning
to run high, and in a lesser degree against the King.
Their surroundings are entirely germanophile, and
this is supposed to be against the grain of the
people. . . ."

On May 22 information that the enemy submarines
had penetrated into the Mediterranean and might
shortly be expected on the scene, invested the situation with a new and most unwelcome aspect.

Defence against this latest weapon of maritime
warfare was still in an embryonic stage, and the fleet

of transports and supply ships which for a whole month had lain unmolested off Helles and Anzac, out of range of the enemy's guns, pouring forth their contents on to the beach, had now to seek safety from his torpedoes in the shelter of Mudros harbour. Henceforth everything—men and stores—had first to be taken to Mudros and there transshipped into small craft, in which we were woefully deficient, for conveyance to the Peninsula, rendering the work of supply more protracted and laborious. The Commander-in-Chief and his Staff could no longer remain afloat, moving as convenient from one scene to another, but had for the same reason to be disembarked. The Peninsula itself was judged impossible as a locality for his headquarters, and the place chosen was Kephalo, a harbour in the island of Imbros, 13 miles distant from Helles, 17 from Anzac, and 55 from Mudros. The necessity of defending it from submarine attack was a further strain on our slender resources, and its separation from the scene of action and from the base, though insuperable, caused inevitable delay of communications in spite of a complete system of telegraph wires and a regular ferry service carried out by trawlers.

" May 23, 1915. . . . I am much rejoiced by the receipt of a wire to-day from the Admiralty saying they are sending me out the *Europa* as a depôt ship. At last ! I sincerely hope there may be some men with her. The Turks make occasional attacks, but are always driven off. Modern warfare leaves but little room for strategy. Armies get held up in long lines in face of each other and there seems no way out of it, except by seeing who can kill most men in the quickest manner possible. ——, who ought to know, thinks that the Turks won't go on much longer. He says that their hearts are not in it, and that they cannot stand being perpetually hammered. I trust it may be so, but I can see no signs of their giving way yet. Nothing here is very exciting; much work, but of a dull nature. I am setting up a canteen on the lines of an open-air club for the men. They must get rest and recreation, as they have a hard and trying time on board their ships."

"May 25, 1915. . . . Yesterday being Empire Day I dined with some Australians who are in camp here. Much speechifying and a nice and somewhat subdued tone throughout them all. It was by no means unpleasing. . . . We have just heard for certain that Fisher and Churchill have actually gone. We must now pray that some sympathy and common sense may be brought to bear on our matters out here. . . ."

The submarine threat materialized on May 25, when the *Triumph* was sunk. This ship had been stationed off Gaba Tepe ever since the first landing where she had been performing good service in affording gun support to the Australian and New Zealand forces. At about half-past twelve that afternoon she was steaming slowly along the coast in a southerly direction with her torpedo nets out and her light guns manned, escorted by the destroyer *Chelmer*, when what was apparently the wash of a submarine was seen some 500 yards off on the starboard beam. The *Chelmer* headed for the suspected craft at full speed in the hopes of ramming her and the *Triumph* instantly opened fire, but was almost immediately struck by a torpedo which hit her nearly amidships and gave her a heavy list.

From the very first it was evident that the ship was doomed, and the *Chelmer*, beautifully handled, came up under her stern walk and succeeded in getting a large number of her crew off, before she capsized only some eight minutes after she had been hit. Many small craft hurried to the scene and, owing to the fine discipline prevailing, only three officers and twenty men were lost when, after lying bottom up for half an hour, she slowly went down stern in the air and disappeared from sight amidst the cries of farewell from the survivors.

Following closely on the loss of the *Triumph* came that of the *Majestic*, two days later, by the same means. The attack was well planned and well carried out. The ship was anchored close off the beach, surrounded by innumerable small craft, and the commander of the submarine must have regularly stalked her. The material loss of these two ships was not in itself of supreme importance and the loss of life but slight, but the moral effect was considerable and infused the Turkish army, which we now know had been somewhat demoralized by its heavy losses since the opening of the campaign, with fresh courage. It also created considerable administrative difficulties, owing to lack of accommodation for the survivors, as had been the case two months before with the crews of *Irresistible* and *Ocean*.

" May 30, 1915. . . . I see that Jackson relieves Fisher. On the whole I think it is the best possible appointment, but I cannot enthuse over A. J. B. as First Lord. At present we know nothing of the circumstances under which these changes have been brought about. I conclude that the Coalition Cabinet is the precursor of conscription. Certainly national organization is what is required and conscription seems the easiest, or rather the least difficult manner of bringing it about. Here the situation remains unchanged. I suppose the Admiralty and War Office have at length grasped that it is no little picnic that they have undertaken. I already see signs of a tendency to give us more assistance. Churchill's name will be handed down to posterity as that of a man who undertook an operation of whose requirements he was entirely ignorant. Of Fisher, I will not speak. . . . Here, I am settled down to the somewhat monotonous but by no means easy task of keeping the army going. My duties are extraordinarily varied ; nothing seems to come amiss, and the subjects to which I have to give my attention would astonish you. Civil administration, naval administration, transport, wounded, secret service, water works, piers, etc. ; the list seems endless and the work amplifies. The soldiers are curious, many of them seem absolutely incapable of assimilating their ideas to their surroundings. They cannot understand that conditions afloat are different to conditions on shore and their demands upon the navy are incessant, often ridiculous, and I am almost sorry to say, nearly always met. Those in the trenches are quite magnificent. . . . One has always to be at concert pitch to keep things going, and it is rather tiring. One has to bear in mind that the Fleet consists of vague ships brought together and that they have never had the chance of being quietly organized as one whole ; that they have not got that invaluable asset of having worked together before. I wish I could write and discuss subjects other than the war, but the fact is that this state of affairs demands the whole of one's energies and the whole of one's thoughts and never does one's brain get the chance of a little change. The enemy, confound him, is the perpetual goal to which one's whole attention is turned. It is five weeks to-day since we landed the army and beyond being firmly established on the Peninsula, we are very little further than we were then. More men—more men—that is always the cry. . . . From all I hear the Australians are an odd mixture, in some situations quite magnificent, in others hopeless. Full of dash and resource they are as yet but imperfectly disciplined, though I believe a great deal better than they were. Of course there are of all sorts among them—land-owners, barristers, architects, adventurers, miners, loafers—all are jostling one another in their ranks and the Colonel of one of the regiments has all his life been a schoolmaster. It must be difficult to get such a jumble of humanity to think on anything like the same plane. Do you know that, except for glancing through the *Morning Post*, in a very perfunctory way, I have not read a newspaper for nearly two months nor a magazine nor a book ! What on earth shall I be like when I return to civilized life again ? . . ."

Every hour's delay was militating in favour of the enemy, giving him time to improve his positions and to bring up reinforcements from Constantinople, which he was able to do in spite of the good work performed by our submarines in the Sea of Marmora, where they were having no inconsiderable success in attacking the sea lines of communication. The necessity of pushing on was consequently imperative, and so the Commander-in-Chief, taking advantage of the arrival of fresh drafts at the end of May, planned a further attack to be delivered on June 4.

On this occasion the Fleet was not called upon for artillery assistance. The submarine menace had rendered it inadvisable for ships to lie off the Peninsula, unless the advantage to be gained from their co-operation was of sufficient importance to be worth the risk entailed. Experience had amply proved that this was not so, for guns of flat trajectory are but of little use in attacking entrenchments and entanglements, especially when there are no means of spotting the fall of the shells as was the case in the present instance. Moreover a fixed gun platform, so important a factor for accurate shooting, was unobtainable owing to movements of the ships being a necessary precaution against submarine attack. In the battle of June 4 there was some very heavy fighting in which the Naval Division suffered severely. The ultimate result was a gain of a few hundred yards, bringing us in effect no real advantage, and after heavy casualties on both sides the situation remained practically the same as it had been before.

" June 9, 1915. . . . I have not seen any of the Headquarters Staff since the battle of the 4th, so I don't know the latest ideas on the business, but one thing is absolutely certain, and that is, that it is going to be an extremely long job. The situation has been misjudged ; probably that mistake, like so many others, emanates from England. . . . De Robeck and I have fallen into the right lines as regards each other. I must confess that it was a sacrifice so far as I was concerned, but I feel quite sure that I did the right thing and that now all is for the best. The loss of the *Triumph* and the *Majestic* are two of those instances of warfare against which it is impossible to guarantee. Luckily the loss of life was small and a fine discipline was maintained. The Captain of the *Triumph* is now my Chief of the Staff and of immense assistance. . . . Our submarines out here have done splendidly. The officers handle their boats magnificently. Had our torpedoes at the commencement of the war been as good as they should have been, there would have been a very different story to tell now. The Greek elections are to take place within a few days, and it is regarded as a certainty that Venizelos will be returned with a large majority. German money is flowing like water throughout the country for the purposes of pro-German propaganda, and the result is very noticeable just now in the tone of the Greek press. An important factor is the serious illness of the King. I am told by a man who ought to know that the election is being looked upon very much in the light of a personal fight between him and Venizelos, and that the danger in which the former lies will very likely have the effect of making many people who would ordinarily have voted for Venizelos, now refrain from doing so because it would be anti-King : an odd psychological fact not very understandable to the non-Greek mind. They are a curious race, the Greeks, but in a way patriotic."

" June 11, 1915. . . . I don't think I am quite as popular with my ' subjects ' as I was. I have had to take very drastic steps with regard to the drinking shops which they don't like, but with a mixed military population like this, one has to take every kind of precaution. . . ."

" June 14. . . . The Greek elections are taking place to-day, and we are all wondering whether there

will be a change of policy if Venizelos is returned.
It is Bulgaria that I want to see coming in on our
side. She is the one whose help would be invaluable
to us."

The eagerly awaited *Europa* arrived on the 15th,
and no time was lost in transferring to her myself
and my Staff, hitherto painfully cramped. To the
latter was the change especially beneficial, giving
them space in which to carry out their work. Matters were further ameliorated by the appointment of
Captain Fitzmaurice, late of the *Triumph*, as my
Chief of the Staff, and henceforth many of the difficulties from which we had hitherto suffered began to
be alleviated.

" June 19. . . . How splendid are the regimental
officers and the rank and file ! They are indeed
heroes. What stuff there is in the ordinary English-
man, if people only knew how to get it out of him !
Of course there are exceptions : where are there not ?
But, thank God, they are so few and far between,
that they only help to throw the others into high
relief. . . . To be pessimistic is foolish, to be optimistic may lead to bad results, so that one has to try
and keep a level head and just go on doing one's job
to the best of one's ability. To-day a long and
interesting letter from Gibson Bowles in which he
says : ' I think we *must* now press on to success and
to Constantinople. The consequences of failure
throughout the East—*our* East—would be ruinous
to us.' "

The situation at the front underwent no material
change during the month of June, in spite of two not
unsuccessful fights on the 21st and 28th. In the
latter the *Talbot*, protected by a screen of destroyers,

rendered considerable aid on our left flank, where she was able to enfilade the enemy's trenches, and our left was advanced from Ghurka Point to Fusilier Bluff. The enemy counter-attacked heavily for two nights in succession, but failed to dislodge our men from their newly won positions and suffered very heavy casualties. All military opinion agreed in believing that in the fight of the 28th it was only the shortage of shell that prevented the attack from being pushed forward, even to the capture of Achi-Baba. But with this shortage, no gallantry could achieve more than the gain of a few hundred yards. Constant counter-attacks on the part of the enemy did nothing to militate against the day's success, but the Allies sustained a great loss by the severe wounding of General Gouraud on the 30th. He was not actually struck by a projectile, but was blown into the air as the result of an 8-inch shell bursting within a few yards of him and his arm and thigh were broken in his fall. General Gouraud, one of France's most brilliant leaders, had succeeded General d'Amade in the command of the French forces only on May 12th, and thus did the Allies lose the services of a great soldier, creating a void difficult to fill.

" June 25, 1915. . . . The weather is very hot, which perhaps helps the work to go slower and gives me much trouble to make other people keep their tempers. Not that they lose them really, but heat always magnifies molehill troubles into mountainous difficulties. , . . I can't tell you what an extraordinary job I have fallen into. I seem to have my finger into every sort of pie that ever was baked. It is a great experience. . . . The military staff here seem quite incapable of grasping the fact that the sea and dry land are two different elements. . . . A man said to me the other day : ' The greatest honour that could be given to an officer would be to make him an honorary private,' and I quite agree with him. They are magnificent. . . ."

" June 29, 1915. . . . The weather is beginning to get very hot and one longs for a thunderstorm and rain. I am afraid the troops must feel it a bit, but they are splendid and fighting magnificently. There was quite a big affair yesterday, when we did well and everybody seems pleased. . . . The Greek Government is behaving very badly on the subject of contraband, full of promises and protestations which they take good care not to carry out—that is truly Greek. We caught a female spy on the high seas the other day. Poor devil ! I am rather sorry for her, for she has to be on board a ship, the only woman until we can get her to Malta. . . . The Ægean Sea is a perfect paradise for the smuggler and illegal trader, and to add to our difficulties, the Greek Government have for years and years never paid any attention to the many illegalities that go on. For instance, about 80 per cent. of the trading ships have no papers, which is quite illegal and acts in favour of the enemy. However, we are gradually hunting the gentlemen down and the harbour is getting quite full of prizes. . . . I go and see some of the wounded whenever I can spare the time, but that is very seldom. I am full of admiration for them, they are so patient and so plucky. They have a bad time of it, as there is that 60 miles of sea for them to cross before they can find themselves properly looked after. . . ."

" June 30, 1915. . . . A great change has come

about since the advent of Balfour and Jackson. That sympathy non-existent before and so essential a factor of success seems to be returning. . . . The Turks have been having a bad time of it of late. The Sea of Marmora has been almost denuded of shipping by our submarines, who have done splendidly. Their losses, too, have been far greater than ours, and one shudders when one thinks of the fate of their wounded. It is a beastly war, but out here it is being waged in a much more respectable manner than anywhere, as far as I can see. . . . "

Owing to Sir Ian Hamilton's urgent represent-ations that victory was unattainable without a far larger number of troops than those at his disposal, the Government early in June decided to reinforce him with three more divisions. Their expected arrival brought about a fresh outburst of activity at Mudros, where at last the necessity of piers and encampments became apparent to the military mind. Camps, hospitals and hutments began to spring up on the shores of the vast harbour, Decauville railways to be laid and piers to be erected with feverish hurry. But the military command at the base was hardly organized in accordance with these large additions, and there resulted a constant change of plans not calculated to produce efficiency. The Admiralty, on their side, were in no ways behindhand and sent out craft suitable for the campaign. Old cruisers and new monitors fitted with "bulges" as protection against torpedoes began to arrive and proved ex-tremely useful ; and to gladden our hearts, a number of motor lighters especially built for carrying troops and horses. These lighters were flat-bottomed and fitted with a special gangway which, on their taking

the shore, were let down from the bows to the beach.
They were capable of carrying 400 men or forty
horses at a time, and proved most suitable for all
sorts of work. What would we not have given to
have possessed some on April 25 !

" July 4, 1915. . . . The heat here is beginning
to be very great, and I trust the troops won't suffer.
So far they seem all right, but the work is ever increasing and we are short of officers and men and
matters are not easy. However, war itself is not an
easy matter, so one must make the best of it. I am
not sure that even now the Admiralty grasp the
magnitude of the operation. The side shows, so to
speak, are so complicated, and the soldiers do not
seem able to grasp the fact that the sea is not dry
land and that the conditions of the two are not the
same. I am beginning at times to long for a day or
two when I should be able to think of nothing and
put the war to one side altogether for forty-eight
hours. However, it is no use letting such thoughts
enter one's head. I am afraid that a year of warfare
is taking its toll of many men, not only in the battle-
field but in the matter of health as well. My latest
interest is the erection of a distilling plant for making
fresh water. The Admiralty have sent out the plant,
but nobody to erect it, so I have had to commandeer
all sorts of strange men from Alexandria, mostly
Russian Jews, to put it up. . . . Oh Lord ! how sick
I am beginning to get of the sight of the arid hills of
this place—not that I have much time for contemplating them. I hear that the amount of German
money circulating in Greece is prodigious. Personally I should like to see Greece go in against us. I
should have the greatest satisfaction in kicking every

Greek out of this island and hoisting the Union Jack. They are a strange race, absolutely untrustworthy and very fickle, and in this they differ in nowise from their ancestors. Of the docility, however, of the islanders I have nothing to complain. . . ."

The first detachments of the new reinforcements arrived on July 10 in the *Aquitania*. Such had been the secrecy surrounding the movements of this huge vessel and the 6,000 troops she carried, that the Admiralty had not even informed me of the date when she might be expected. Hence, when she arrived off the entrance of the harbour in the early morning while it was still quite dark, we were unprepared for her reception. The gate of the net-defence was of course closed, and the delay in opening it, slight though it was, forced her to stop and thus offer an easy target to any submarines hovering about, as day broke, in search of just such a prey. The relief I felt on getting her safely into harbour was great enough almost to compensate for the few minutes of intense anxiety caused by the danger she had undergone.

" July 13, 1915. . . . A particular and extra burst of much to do. The weather, too, is getting very hot, which does not add to the general comfort ; however, I manage to keep my temper, though there is much to try it. The soldiers are trying, for they never are of the same mind for two seconds running. Perhaps this would not much matter if there were only terra firma to deal with, but when all the transport is over sea and ships limited, it *is* trying. To keep smiling and to do what one can is the only way, but God bless me, I had rather have to do with a dozen rogues who know what they want, than with one angel who doesn't. Lord bless me, what a mess we, or rather the authorities at home, have made of it all. . . . The latest thing I have put myself to do is to try and stop these beastly Greeks from depreciating the French paper money, but I don't suppose I shall succeed because the limit of my authority is so circumscribed. I have an idea of seizing all the merchandise in the place and putting a price on it ; I think also of expelling any merchant who refuses to give par for French paper ; but behind it all, I have the feeling that I should only be kicking against the pricks. I am trying to enlist the services of our Minister at Athens on my behalf, but I fear he will not be able to help. . . . I rather shudder when I think how terribly parochial I must be getting in my ideas. Lemnos ! ! That at present is my limit. . . ."

" July 21, 1915. . . . You can't think how complicated is this machine, and however successfully one complication may be dealt with and straightened out, there is always another one at the end of it. Of course in war one has to be ready for sudden and lightning changes, but I can't think that the army at Mudros really try to make easier our very difficult task. We are always tearing our very insides out to help them—not for their own sakes, *bien entendu*, but for the sake of the general welfare of us all—but they never appear to think that there is anything of that sort due from them to us. Perhaps I don't thoroughly appreciate their position and do them a wrong in thus judging them, but I don't think I do. To-day I managed to find time to go and see some of the wounded. I am full of admiration for them, so patient and so grateful for anything one can do for

them. Luckily the sea is smooth and the weather
fine, so that they have not got the extra agony of
sea-sickness to contend with. At first the medical
arrangements were shocking, but they are better
now. Getting them away from the Peninsula is not
an easy job. Poor fellows ! I believe they are so
delighted at getting into the peace and quiet of a
hospital, be it ashore or afloat, that they forget half
their agonies."

" July 23, 1915. . . . Generals seem to spring
up like mushrooms in the night, and each one's Staff
seems to be more glittering than the last ; I hope
their usefulness is in like proportion. . . . Works
of all sorts are going on, which must eventually largely
benefit the inhabitants who, being wily Greeks, will
make every use of their opportunities. . . . I gather
that the English public are somewhat depressed, not
that there is anything to be depressed about, only
they have been lured on by false insinuations to hope
for great things which cannot come off. The people
latest out from England are raging against North-
cliffe and Lloyd George who, they tell me, are bound
up together. God ! What I feel about the politicians ! The other day there was an armistice on
the Peninsula to bury the dead : while it was going
on a Turkish officer strolled up to our lines and found
a chaplain reading the service over a large grave.
When it was finished, he took off his fez, looked down
into the grave and said in a loud voice : ' God bless
all true soldiers and eternally damn all politicians.'
The Turks are a brave enemy and have fought
cleanly all through. . . ."

At the end of July there arrived General Altham
to assume the command of the line of communi-

cations, and from this time on the military position at the base underwent a rapid change for the better. Method and order took the place of disorganization and confusion, and I now found myself with a responsible military colleague with whom I was able to work hand in hand with the greatest cordiality and co-operation. The delay in sending out such an officer was but another proof of the lack of appreciation of our necessities hitherto reigning in Government circles at home and of the want of foresight.

With him came Admiral Gamble, for the purpose of reporting to the Admiralty on the naval situation with regard to boats, vessels, etc. His arrival was most welcome, for I could give him ocular demonstration of the difficulties arising from the great shortage of small craft worth hundreds of written reports and telegrams. Not that the Admiralty had been unsympathetic in the matter, indeed they were helping to the utmost of their power, but they too were handicapped by the original want of vision and the lee-way was difficult to make up.

There also arrived at this time Surgeon-General Sir James Porter, appointed by the Admiralty with the consent of the War Office to supervise the oversea transport of the wounded.

The arrangements for dealing with them had from the very outset been inadequate, chiefly owing—as was the case with most of our troubles—to the original under-estimation of our requirements.

When the expedition started from Mudros on April 23, it was fully recognized that it was improbable that any attention would be paid to the wounded on the first day until nightfall, when it was hoped that it would be possible to convey all the cases to the hospital ships lying off the beaches ready for their reception, and for this purpose ship's launches had been suitably prepared, but it soon became distressingly evident that the preparation had been made on a totally inadequate scale.

As a result of the failure of the army to advance more than a few hundred yards after landing, the establishment of field hospitals on the Peninsula was out of the question, creating almost insurmountable difficulties in attending to the wounded before they were sent back for embarkation. The condition of the wounded, therefore, when they arrived on the beaches was pitiful and their numbers far greater than could properly be dealt with. Every available boat was requisitioned for taking them off to the hospital ships, quickly filled to overflowing. The men-of-war took on board all that they could deal with, and still there were many who could find no asylum. Boats full of suffering men went from ship to ship seeking accommodation that could not be found, and though empty transports were used to shelter them, they had neither doctors nor medical equipment. Seeing how matters stood, I made an offer to Surgeon-General Birrel, the Director of Military Services, of as many naval surgeons as could be spared from the Fleet, with the necessary proviso that he must be prepared to allow them to return to their ships immediately, should the necessity arise, for at that time there was no foreseeing what duties the men-of-war might be called upon quickly to undertake.

I was a good deal shocked when my offer was refused, on account, as the Surgeon-General explained, of the attached condition making it impossible for him to find suitable work for them to do.   I was unable to acquiesce in his refusal and went personally to see Sir Ian Hamilton—at that time afloat in the *Arcadian*, to protest against the refusal to make use of available help.   My protest had the desired effect ;   some fourteen naval surgeons were distributed amongst the doctorless ships, thus at least temporarily filling a void.

All this happened in the very early days.   The shortage of hospital ships and of medical equipment was soon remedied, but the inconvenience arising from the want of hospitals on the Peninsula and the difficulties due to the separation of the base from the fighting line by 60 miles of water were never got rid of ;   indeed they considerably increased when in May the submarine menace rendered obligatory for the transport of the wounded the use of small vessels of light draft which, on account of their many and multifarious other duties, could not be properly fitted up as carriers.

However, time, experience and goodwill all helped towards an amelioration.

CHAPTER VII

WITH the promise of three more full divisions,
together with another two of infantry, the
outlook assumed a more promising aspect than it
had worn at any time since the first check encountered after the landing of April 25. With the addition of these reinforcements the Commander-in-
Chief was enabled to undertake fresh operations of
a wider and more comprehensive scope than anything
the number of troops hitherto at his disposal had
yet admitted of.

The strategical conception of Sir Ian Hamilton's
plan was:

(1) To break out with a rush from Anzac and cut
off the bulk of the Turkish army from land communications with Constantinople.

(2) To gain such a command for our artillery as
to cut off the bulk of the Turkish army from sea-
traffic both with Constantinople and Asia.

(3) To secure Suvla Bay as a winter base for Anzac
and all the troops operating in the Northern theatre.

It will be seen, then, that though no co-ordinated
part of the military operations, the submarine warfare waged against the enemy's lines of communication in the Sea of Marmora from April to December
played a conspicuous part in the general offensive.

In spite of difficulties that might well have been
considered insurmountable our submarine commanders succeeded in penetrating the defences of the

Narrows and by their assaults on the enemy's shipping created a veritable panic in these waters, hitherto regarded by him as safe. Battleships, cruisers, gunboats, transports, supply vessels of every description all were attacked with a cool courage and calculated audacity unsurpassed even in the annals of our own naval history. Only in this theatre of the war did these officers find a full outlet for their prowess and initiative ; and they proved that this latest weapon of maritime warfare could be effectively used in a manner very different to that exercised by the Germans in their merciless campaign against allied and neutral shipping, for though our officers did not hesitate to sink enemy's vessels they never did so without ascertaining that they were legitimate targets, whilst they scrupulously respected the lives of non-combatants.

The first officer to negotiate the mine barrage at Chanak was Lieut.-Commander Norman Holbrook. In December, 1914, he dived his boat B 11 under the mines and succeeded in sinking the Turkish cruiser *Messudieh*, thereby opening out a prospect of future possibilities that were made the most of later on.

Submarine E 15 was the next to attempt the perilous exploit. How she ran ashore in the Straits and was eventually destroyed by Lieut.-Commander Robinson and thus prevented from falling into the hands of the enemy has already been related. A E 2, Lieut.-Commander Stocker, was more successful. On April 25, whilst the first attack was in progress, she passed up the Straits and sunk a Turkish gunboat, only unhappily to meet a similar fate at the hands of an enemy torpedo boat five days later.

The experience gained by these early successes

was a great encouragement to further action, and raised hopes, subsequently to be fully realized, of so seriously interfering with the Turkish army's lines of communication as materially to hamper its movements on the Peninsula.

On April 27, Lieut.-Commander Boyle in E 14 after a passage through the Straits, in which he encountered gun-fire, commenced a raid that lasted for three weeks and resulted in the sinking of a gunboat and two transports; one of the latter carried no less than 6,000 men, all of whom perished. Others she chased back into Constantinople and eventually, when she had fired all her torpedoes, returned on May 18, after having been attacked by patrol vessels so continuously as to make the possibility of recharging the batteries a matter of perpetual anxiety.

Lieut.-Commander Nasmith now took up the task. His vessel, E 11, was armed with a 6-pounder gun that considerably increased the scope of his activities, enabling him as it did to deal with small craft without an undue expenditure of torpedoes.

Rounding Kilid Bahr point on the early morning of May 19 he came across a Turkish battleship and several destroyers that immediately opened fire on his periscope and then fled northward. Two days later, having overhauled a small sailing ship, he lashed his vessel alongside of her and, thus disguised, cruised all day off Constantinople on the look out for transports without however obtaining any success. On the 23rd he torpedoed a Turkish gunboat lying at anchor off that city, who, before sinking, opened fire and hit his periscope necessitating a retreat to unfrequented waters to repair the damage inflicted.

Two days later he returned and diving into the very waters of Constantinople, torpedoed a large transport lying alongside the Arsenal. But in effecting his retreat he very nearly came to grief through the submarine grounding heavily and experiencing considerable difficulty in extricating herself from the cross currents of those narrow waters.

During this cruise of nineteen days' duration three more transports, an ammunition ship, and a small steamer were destroyed. In connection with the latter, there occurred an incident as comic as it was unexpected. Examination showed that she was carrying guns and other warlike stores, and before she was blown up the crew were ordered to abandon her. In their haste to comply some of the boats were capsized, though no lives were lost, and in the midst of the confusion that ensued a figure appeared on the upper deck which after proclaiming itself to be Mr. Silas Q. Swing, correspondent of the *Chicago Sun,* assured the somewhat astonished submarine commander that he was pleased to make his acquaintance!

Nor was this the only instance of absence of hostile feeling encountered, for with the crew of a sailing vessel whose cargo was found to be innocent Nasmith relates that " they parted with many expressions of good will on both sides."

Minor machinery defects necessitated a return to the base on June 7. During the passage through the Narrows at a depth of 70 feet a shock was felt which, had such not been impossible in that locality, would have indicated that the vessel had bumped the ground heavily. On rising to a depth of 20 feet for the purpose of investigation a large mine was found to be hung up by its moorings to the stern of the submarine.   To clear it whilst submerged was impossible ; to come to the surface would have exposed the ship to the fire of the shore batteries ; and so for a whole hour was the passage continued in contact with an instrument of destruction that at any moment might have exploded and brought the career of these gallant men to an untimely end. It was not until Kum-Kale had been passed that E 11 was brought to the surface and by clever manœuvring freed from its unwelcome companion.

For three days only was the shipping plying between Constantinople and the Peninsula to have any respite from attack.   On June 10 Boyle, now a Commander, successfully negotiated the hazardous passage of the Narrows for the second time, to be followed ten days later by E 12 (Lieut.-Commander Bruce) and E 7 (Lieut.-Commander Cochrane), and from henceforth until the very end of the campaign the Turkish *mare clausum* was the scene of uninterrupted raids on shipping, of attacks on railways, viaducts and even bodies of troops, that caused consternation to the enemy and a very serious check to the supply and reinforcement of his army on the Peninsula.

Thoroughly alarmed by the success of these operations, the Turks sought, but sought in vain, to close the entrance of the Marmora by laying across the Straits at Nagara an anti-submarine net watched by patrol vessels and defended by specially erected batteries.   But it proved unavailing, and our submarines continued their incursions unhindered by this new obstruction.

Commander Boyle was the first to show that it

was ineffective. After a three-weeks rest at Mudros
he started off for his third cruise on July 21. Scrap-
ing past a mine near Kephaz, he hit off the only gap
in the net, a narrow gate purposely left to allow a
passage for enemy vessels, and continued his attacks
for another three weeks. On his return, however,
on August 12, he was less fortunate and missing the
gate, charged into the net. For twenty seconds,
which must have seemed like twenty hours to her
devoted crew, the submarine, brought from a depth
of 80 feet to 40 feet, laboured in its meshes and
then crashed through. But even then the dangers
were not yet passed. She came under the fire of
the batteries of Kilid Bahr, was the target of a
torpedo from Chanak and almost immediately
afterwards bumped a mine; but with the good
fortune that surely was the due of so much devotion,
skill and gallantry on the part of her crew, she
triumphantly survived all these perils and once more
gained the safety of Mudros Harbour.

In the meantime Nasmith had left the base on
August 5 to join Boyle. Before reaching Nagara
he encountered another new obstacle in the form
of a wire hawser stretched between two buoys
apparently laid out for the purpose of damaging a
periscope if not entirely stopping a submarine. No
damage, however, was sustained, but almost immediately afterwards he bumped a mine which happily
proved ineffective. By diving to 110 feet he hoped
to pass under the net, but although he did not
succeeded in avoiding it, he pushed his way through
without harm and ten minutes afterwards torpedoed
a transport lying in Ak-Baschi Liman. The following day E 14 was met by arrangement, and whilst

the two Commanders were still conferring the smoke of an approaching steamer was observed on the horizon. The boats spread to attack and an hour later E 11 torpedoed what proved to be a gunboat that was eventually beached to avoid sinking. Five days later E 14 returned to the base under the circumstances just related and E 11 continued her cruise. During the next twelve days she three times attacked troops marching along the road to Gallipoli, scattering the columns and causing many casualties ; she torpedoed the battleship *Harridin Barkaressa,* which capsized half an hour after she had been hit ; she burnt six small sailing craft ; went to Constantinople, where she sank a transport alongside the Haidar Pacha railway pier ; bombarded a viaduct of the Bagdad Railway in the Gulf of Ismid ; stopped and examined two hospital ships and was twice ineffectually attacked by aeroplanes, to one of which Nasmith derisively waved before diving to avoid its bombs.

Along the north coast of the Gulf of Ismid runs the railway line connecting Constantinople with Asia Minor, and this Nasmith and Lieutenant D'Oyly Hughes, his second in command, determined to render unserviceable by blowing up a viaduct across a ravine not far from the sea-shore. To carry out this plan E 11 arrived in the Gulf in the evening of August 20, and at 2 a.m. on the following morning, whilst still quite dark, the vessel was trimmed down until the conning tower only was above water and slowly manœuvred towards the shore till her stem grounded within a few yards of the rocks at a spot where the cliffs on either side were of sufficient height to prevent the conning tower being observed. D'Oyly Hughes, who had volunteered to make the attempt, then quietly dropped into the water and pushed a small raft constructed for the purpose of holding the demolition charge, his clothes, a revolver and a sharpened bayonet to a spot some 60 yards distant, where he meant to land. The cliffs here proving unclimbable, he swam along the coast with his raft to a more favourable place, scrambled up the cliffs, dressed and reached the railway. Nobody was about and he walked along the line in the direction of the viaduct for some 600 yards when he suddenly heard voices. Three men were sitting on the line between him and his goal. Laying down the heavy and cumbersome demolition charge, he made a wide detour to reconnoitre, stumbling into a poultry yard on the way, only finally to discover the viaduct guarded. Any attempt to blow it up had perforce to be abandoned, and quickly changing his plans he placed the demolition charge under a neighbouring culvert 150 yards distant from the three men first sighted. In spite of his attempts to deaden the sound of the firing of the fuse pistol, its noise rang through the still night and aroused the watchers. Realizing that any attempt to effect his escape over the cliffs could only lead to capture, D'Oyly Hughes ran down the railway as fast as he could, stopping once or twice to turn and fire his revolver at the three men who were in hot pursuit. A mile brought him to a point where the line came out close to the shore and here he took to the water. As he did so the charge exploded. His pre-concerted signal of a long blast on a whistle failed to reach the ears anxiously awaiting it and he was forced to swim back to the shore to rest himself.

But the day was fast breaking and there was no time to be lost, so once more he plunged into the sea and this time the signal was heard. As the submarine backed out of the little cove in which she had been lying hidden, the morning mist gave her conning tower and gun the appearance of two fishing boats and D'Oyly-Hughes, believing himself trapped, returned to the rocks. Quickly realizing, however, his mistake, he went in a third time and was eventually picked up in an exhausted condition. And only just in time, for daylight had revealed his presence to his pursuers who opened fire before he reached the submarine which, having got him safely on board, dived out of the sight of the baffled enemy.

E 11's next exploit was an encounter with a convoy consisting of three tugs and several sailing vessels in the charge of a destroyer. They were met at night and followed until daylight, when, the destroyer dropping astern to render assistance to one of the tugs that had broken down, Nasmith seized the opportunity of attacking the others. Rising to the surface as soon as out of range of the destroyer's guns he inflicted severe damage on one of the two remaining tugs and on several of the sailing vessels before being forced to dive by the return of the destroyer. The subsequent wild movements of the thoroughly flustered vessels enabled him eventually to sink the broken-down tug and one of the sailing ships whose crew of twenty men jumped overboard at the first shot. They were all picked up and made prisoners and later on in the day placed on board another ship after they had willingly enough discharged her cargo into the sea, pleased and surprised at their lives being spared. One of their number was a stout German bank-manager carrying a large sum of money to Chanak. This, in the first excitement of the attack, he had thrown overboard, and when he realized that he was to escape with his life his lamentations over his lost treasure were loud and long. As he floated away from the submarine on a lifebuoy, his ample proportions scantily clad in a short pink silk jersey, the spectacle afforded to the amused crew of E 11 was one not easily to be forgotten by them.

During the next twelve days nine more sailing vessels were burnt or otherwise destroyed and four more large steamers sunk; the latter all on the same day and within the space of a few hours. Two of them were sent to the bottom by torpedoes fired simultaneously from the two bow tubes, whilst the fourth succumbed to E 11's last missile.

The viaduct on the Ismid railway that had escaped destruction at the hands of D'Oyly-Hughes on August 24 was subjected to an hour's bombardment from a position just out of range of guns since brought to defend it : a bombardment only brought to an end by the advent of another gun outranging that of the submarine, not however before the bridge had been frequently hit and sustained considerable damage. The railway station at Mudania and an adjacent magazine were also targets for E 11 and E 2 operating together, and the four weeks' eventful cruise was brought to an end on September 3 by a successful charge through the Nagara net which, though checking the vessel's way, did not succeed in stopping her homeward career.

But the net hitherto unsuccessful was soon to claim a victim. On the next day, September 4,

E 7, Lieut.-Commander Cochrane, was caught in it. For more than twelve hours did she struggle to disentangle herself from its meshes, subjected all the while to bombs of the patrolling vessels. Rising eventually to the surface she was still unable to get free and was sunk by Cochrane himself after all the crew had jumped overboard and been made prisoners.

Notwithstanding this misfortune the other submarines continued their adventurous careers. Two months later the French *Turquoise*, after successfully traversing the Narrows, fell a captive to the enemy and by a tragic fate was destined to lead to the destruction of yet another submarine. She had arranged a meeting at a given rendezvous with E 20, Lieut.-Commander Clifford Warren, for November 6, and a note to that effect was found on board by her captors. There was sufficient time for the enemy to take advantage of this untoward circumstance, and when E 20 arrived at the meeting place she was torpedoed by the German submarine U 14 that was awaiting her arrival.

Nasmith's third and last cruise was commenced on November 7. The conditions prevailing in the Marmora had considerably altered since April. Some of the few surviving steamers were armed; those lying at anchor were surrounded by nets or screens of small craft whilst at many of the anchorages guns had been mounted for their protection. Yet in spite of these precautions, of much bad weather and of the greatly decreased amount of shipping E 11 during the forty-five days that this cruise lasted accounted for no less than eleven steamers, five large sailing vessels and thirty-five smaller ones. Again did Nasmith attack the Ismid railway, setting fire to a wagon of a goods train passing over the now familiar line in the Gulf of Ismid ; again did he dive into the waters of Constantinople and torpedo a steamer lying alongside the quay, where to this day the wondering inhabitants still point out to the passing stranger the marks of the damage inflicted by the British submarine. Another destroyer was sunk of whose crew of eighty-five, two officers and forty men, five being Germans, were rescued. Once more were the bombs of an attacking aeroplane successfully avoided. A gun-action with a despatch vessel was maintained for several hours, ending by the latter being set on fire, and E 11 eventually returned to Mudros on December 23, two days after the evacuation of Suvla and Anzac had been effected.

Thus to the very end of the campaign was the warfare on the enemy's shipping maintained, a warfare that had succeeded in interrupting the supplies of the Turkish army to such an extent as to bring about an almost total abandonment of the sea route.

Of the thirteen submarines that at one time or another sought to force an entrance into the sea of Marmora two British vessels and one French found a glorious end in its waters. Of the five that succeeded and survived E 11 and E 14 were not the only ones whose doings are worthy of being chronicled, but space does not admit of any further description of their acts of prowess in this volume. The history of one and all contains deeds of daring only made possible by technical knowledge of the highest degree, by courage and endurance in its most conspicuous form, by foresight, patience, and perseverance on the part of those officers and men who in the face of unknown dangers and extreme hazards played a part in the campaign second to none in glory and success.

Mine were no empty words when in December I told the Admiralty that the Navy was prepared to cut off all Turkish supplies finding their way to the Peninsula either by sea from the Marmora or across the Dardanelles from the Asiatic shore. The submarines had proved that this was feasible; indeed so far as the Marmora was concerned they had then already practically done so, and this fact must be taken into due consideration before any judgment can be passed on the possibility of the expedition having been brought to another and successful termination.

Though in July the submarine campaign had not yet reached its highest development it had already caused the enemy to abandon the sea route for the transport of troops, thus entailing a delay in bringing reinforcements to the Peninsula that could not but have hampered Liman von Sanders in making his dispositions for meeting the new attack the locality of which he could not foretell. The interval of time that could thus be counted on before the troops landing at Suvla on the night of August 6 were likely to meet with any serious opposition was a dominant factor in our Commander-in-Chief's plans, for in the Northern area there were two separate operations which though distinct from one another were interdependent for subsequent action; the attack from Anzac and the seizure of Suvla Bay.

The break out from Anzac was planned with the object of seizing the heights of Sari Bahr mountain whose capture would have given our artillery the

11

command of the Dardanelles and have made possible
a further advance on the Kilid Bahr plateau from
that direction, whilst the possession of Suvla Bay
was not only desirable from the facilities it would
afford as a base, but was necessary as a place of
disembarkation for the troops that were to co-operate
on the left of the Anzac forces in their attack on
Sari Bahr.

To facilitate the comprehension of the Commander-
in-Chief's plans and of the previous troop movements
that they entailed it will be convenient to give a
brief description of the conditions of affairs before
the attack was launched on the night of August 6.

Our three months' incessant fighting had failed
to procure for us either at Helles or at Anzac sufficient depth of ground to allow the formation of
camps behind the fighting line, and as a consequence
all reserves had to be accommodated at the bases
separated from the area of action by several miles
of water over which they had to be conveyed in
troop-carriers of shallow draft before they could be
brought into the fighting line.   On this occasion,
moreover, sufficient space was not available at
Mudros and Imbros for the extra divisions destined
to take part in the forthcoming operations and six
battalions of the 10th Division were at Mitylene.
From three separate bases, therefore, Mitylene,
Mudros and Imbros, distant from Suvla, 120, 60,
and 15 miles respectively, had large bodies of troops
to be brought punctually to the scene of action over
a route in full view of the enemy and landed on an
open beach commanded by heights in his possession.
Secrecy under such circumstances necessitated that
the opening moves should be made under cover of

darkness and this fact fixed the date to the night of August 6–7 when the moon would rise at 2 a.m.

General Birdwood's force at Anzac was to be reinforced by the 13th Division, a Brigade of the 10th Division and the 29th Indian Division, and these were to be landed at Anzac during the dark hours of the three nights preceding the attack ; but since, as already has been stated, there was no room for camps they all had to be stowed away in concealed bivouacs until the time of action arrived.

The necessary preparations for this secret concentration of force were prodigious, involving the digging of hiding holes, the building of tanks for the storage of water and a large accumulation of provisions and stores, and were carried out by the troops holding the lines. " All the heavy labour was performed by the Australian and New Zealand soldiers almost entirely by night," writes Sir Ian Hamilton in his despatch of December 11, 1915, "and the uncomplaining efforts of the much tried troops in preparation are, in a sense, as much to their credit as their heroism in the battles that followed."

It is a remarkable fact that these preparations, all going forward in a comparatively small space, in full view of an enemy only a few yards distant, should have been conducted without his knowledge, and that so large a number of extra troops should have been so completely hidden away without his realizing their presence. It constitutes a perfection of well-considered measures being carefully and minutely executed seldom if ever accomplished before. Indeed the whole concentration was in itself a complicated operation demanding elaborate and detailed planning on the part of both the naval and military staffs and the closest co-operation between the two Services. " The sheet-anchor on which hung the whole of these elaborate schemes," wrote the Commander-in-Chief, " was the Navy. One tiny flaw in the perfect and mutual trust and confidence animating the two Services would have wrecked the whole enterprise." That a want of co-operation was not the cause of the ill-success of the undertaking must ever be a source of some consolation to those whose carefully prepared work enabled the first part of the operation to be carried out without a hitch.

The Turks were on this occasion confronted by a problem not dissimilar to that which had faced them in April. They knew that large reinforcements had reached us and they were anticipating a further attack, but, as at the original landing, they were unable to foresee the point at which the thrust would be made, the choice of which, owing to the freedom of our sea-communications lay in our hands. This uncertainty was heightened by feints. The presence of considerable forces at Mitylene would, it was hoped, cause apprehension of a landing on the Asiatic coast, off which French men-of-war made demonstrations and carried out reconnaissances. A surprise landing of a small force on the northern shore of the Gulf of Xeros was effected in the hopes of constituting a threat to the Bulair Isthmus; and by a dissemination of false rumours everything was done to oblige the enemy to keep his forces dispersed until the actual point of attack was disclosed.

Surprise being essential for the success of the initial phase, the secrecy maintained as to the time

and place of the attack was carried to such a degree
that many officers were left in ignorance of the
locality fixed upon and even of the nature of the
task before them until they found themselves landed
on the beaches at Suvla ; indeed, the Brigadier commanding the force at Mitylene had no idea either
of his destination or of what he was intended to do
until informed by the captain of the ship in which
he was conveyed to the scene. These stratagems
were completely successful, for when in the early
hours of the morning of August 7 Field-Marshal
Liman von Sanders learnt that troops were being
landed in large numbers on the beaches between
Anzac and Suvla Point, his reserves, amounting to
some 40,000 men, were divided between Bulair and
the Asiatic side of the Straits, and facing the invaders
were only three battalions and some twenty guns.

The 11th Division from Imbros was landed on
the beaches at Suvla during the dark hours of the
night of August 6–7, the operation being greatly
facilitated by the presence of motor-lighters that
had been arriving from England in goodly quantities ever since the month of June. These craft
proved admirably suited to the purpose. Capable
of holding 400 fully equipped men, they were constructed of bullet-proof iron, drew $4\frac{1}{2}$ feet of water,
and in the bows of each was a stout gangboard
capable of being lowered on to the beach when the
lighter took the ground, thus enabling the troops
to reach the shore dry-shod.

The whole of the 11th Division was ashore by
2 a.m., not however without sustaining casualties.
At one of the beaches the water proved too shallow
to allow of the motor-lighters getting close in and

the troops had to wade through 4 feet of water under the fire of snipers concealed in the overlooking heights, so that when the Mitylene contingent arrived punctually to time at daylight some delay was caused by the necessity of finding another more suitable place for landing. The remainder of the 10th Division reached the scene as arranged at 8 a.m., and the disembarkation continued throughout the day, though not with the celerity that had been expected.

The attack from Anzac was opened on the afternoon of the 6th by a heavy bombardment of the enemy's positions from H.M.S. *Bacchante* and two monitors, at the conclusion of which an assault was delivered on his lines by the Australian troops at 4.30 p.m. After two days of incessant fighting, of furious attacks and counter-attacks in this region, a series of formidable positions were captured and remained in our hands.

This offensive, however, was not the main objective, but was undertaken with the purpose of holding the enemy in that quarter whilst some 16,000 of General Birdwood's forces emerged from their hiding-holes and under cover of night made their way in two columns along the beach to attack the heights of Sari Bahr from the westward.

But before this advance could be made with any prospect of success, a position on the enemy's right flank known as Old No. 3 Post had to be taken. " Amongst other stratagems," says the despatch, " the Anzac troops, assisted by H.M.S. *Colne*, had long and carefully educated the Turks how they should lose Old No. 3 Post, which could scarcely have been rushed by simple force of arms. Every night, exactly at 9 p.m., H.M.S. *Colne* threw the beam of

her searchlight on the redoubt and opened fire
upon it for exactly ten minutes. Then after ten
minutes' interval, came a second illumination and
bombardment, commencing always at 9.20 and
ending precisely at 9.30 p.m. The idea was that,
after successive nights of such practices, the enemy
would get into the habit of taking the searchlight
as a hint to clear out until the shelling was at an
end. But on the eventful night of the 6th, the
sound of their footsteps drowned by the loud can-
nonade, unseen as they crept along in the darkest
shadows which fringe a searchlight beam, came the
right covering column. At 9.30 the light switched
off, and instantly our men poured out of the scrub
jungle and into the empty redoubt. By 11 p.m. the
whole series of surrounding entrenchments were ours."

It was calculated that these columns would gain
the crest of the heights by daylight, but the difficulties of a night advance over that rough and
unknown country proved greater than anticipated.
Dense scrub and rocky spurs, only to be climbed
on hands and knees, rendered the advance slow
and fatiguing and the entrances to the ravines were
found to be protected by stiff barbed wire erections
flanked by strongly held trenches that caused many
casualties. When, then, dawn broke on the morning
of the 7th the troops were still far from their goal
and in too exhausted a condition to permit of their
doing anything more than cling to the positions
they had gained, nor were the troops landed during
the night at hand to support them.

The failure of General Stopford's Divisions to
push on after they had landed has been attributed
to various causes, amongst others to shortage of

drinking-water for the troops. The difficulties of supply had not been overlooked, but the arrangements for distribution broke down. " The water problem caused anxiety to the Admiral (J. de Robeck), Lieut.-General Birdwood and myself. The troops to advance from Suvla Bay across the Anafarta valley might reckon on finding some wells—it was certain at least that no water was waiting for us on the crests of the ridges of Sari Bahr. Therefore, first, several days' supply had to be stocked into tanks along the beach and then pumped up into tanks half way up the mountains ; secondly a system of mule transport had to be worked out, so that in so far as was humanly possible thirst should not be allowed to overcome the troops after they had overcome the difficulties of the country and the resistance of the enemy." (Sir Ian Hamilton's despatch.)

The respective responsibilities of the Navy and Army for the supply of water were clearly defined and perfectly understood. It was the duty of the Navy to convey it to the beaches, of the Army to pump it ashore and distribute it. Tank vessels and water lighters accompanied the 11th Division from Imbros, and though some of the water carriers, like the motor lighters, grounded some way out, hoses were laid on to enable the water to be pumped ashore. Neither mules nor water-carts however were landed during the early stages of the disembarkation and it was not until the increasing heat of the day was making itself felt by the troops, already fatigued by their experiences of the night, that the disembarkation of artillery was discontinued in order to hasten the landing of the necessary means of distribution. This delay appears to have had a paralyzing effect on the forward movement of the forces.

There arose at the time some controversy as to whom the blame was attributable. The matter was thoroughly investigated by the Dardanelles Commissioners who reported that the arrangements should have been more thoroughly discussed between the Administrative Staff, at General Headquarters, and the Corps Administrative Staff, and that the Navy had carried out their duties with regard to the supply of sea-borne water in an efficient manner and were always ready to render any assistance in their power. Sir Thomas Mackenzie, one of the Commissioners, in his supplementary report pointed out that " Captain Carver, R.N. (the naval officer in charge of the water-lighters), did his best to encourage prompt action, but this was regarded by the military as undue interference, and he was withdrawn."

Simultaneously with the main operations, a big containing attack was launched on the Helles front. Here, after the usual preliminary bombardment of the enemy's lines the infantry assaulted at 3.30 on the afternoon of the 6th, but in spite of the ardour displayed by our troops no success was achieved. The enemy trenches were found to be packed with troops, as were his communication trenches, on account, as it afterwards transpired, of an attack the Turks themselves were preparing to launch upon us. Fighting raged with varying fortune until the 13th, when, in spite of heavy losses on both sides, the position remained materially unchanged. Though local successes were not achieved, it was claimed that the operation had gained its primary object by preventing the Turks from sending reinforcements to the aid of their troops defending the positions at Sari Bahr.

There is no intention of describing in this narrative the series of obstinate and bloody engagements that ensued in the Northern area. Their success would have placed us in possession of the heights overlooking the Straits and would have facilitated a further naval attack on the forts of the Narrows, even if it had not procured us an immediate victory over the Turkish army; nor is it in its province to deal with the delays occurring at Suvla on August 7 and 8 that frustrated the aims of the Commander-in-Chief. I was ill at the time, confined to my bed by rather a severe attack of dysentery, which under any circumstances would have prevented my following the course of these events; but no naval officer, even had he been on the spot and witnessed all that occurred, could satisfactorily describe the military position as it developed hour by hour during those early days of August. The story has often been told and will often be told again.

By August 16 it was evident that the great attack had failed, and that nothing further would be achieved without large reinforcements. But though all hopes of any decisive issue had perforce to be abandoned, another attempt was made on the 21st to improve our situation by seizing positions that would have secured Suvla Bay and the beaches at Anzac from artillery fire. This battle proved costly, but though unsuccessful in obtaining the desired ground, it did render possible the junction of the Anzac and Suvla forces; and henceforth till the day of the evacuation our line ran continuously from Gaba Tepe to the shores of the Gulf of Xeros at the feet of Kiretch Tepe.

CHAPTER VIII

THESE operations were destined to be the last serious effort undertaken to reach Constantinople and turned out to be the culminating point of the campaign. They had been planned with the object of seizing the heights dominating the Straits and cutting off the Turkish army from its communications, and had they been attended by success, the resistance of the forts of the Dardanelles would have been overcome, the mine-fields destroyed and the passage of the Fleet to Constantinople opened. But they had failed. How close they came to success is now known, and no better testimony can be desired than that given by Field-Marshal Liman von Sanders himself, who in his book *Five Years in Turkey* describes the three critical stages when victory for either side hung in the balance. The first was on the morning of August 7, when our troops seized Kojan Chemin Tepe ; the second, on the morning of the 9th, when, after a counter-attack by the Turks, Mestan Tepe (Scimitar Hill) remained in our hands, only to be retaken by them on the morning of the 10th ; and the third on the 15th, when reinforcements from the Asiatic shores had not arrived in time to prevent our pushing forward to the middle of Kiretch Tepe. The Field-Marshal expresses the opinion that had we attacked Kiretch Tepe a few days earlier, when it was impossible for the Turks to send reinforcements there, the whole Peninsula would have fallen into our hands. The Commanders-in-Chief on either side appear at times to have been confronted by much the same difficulties. On the afternoon of the 7th von Sanders had been informed that the 16th (Turkish) Corps after a forced march from the Gulf of Xeros were ready for an attack in the Anafarta sphere. Our disembarkation was then rapidly proceeding and our troops spreading out to the northward. The Field-Marshal therefore ordered an attack to be delivered on both sides of the Asmak Dere on the morning of the 8th by this 16th Corps, and himself went before daylight to the place where he expected to see these troops, only to learn that they could not possibly arrive in time to attack as ordered. The attack was consequently postponed till after sunset, when, under the pretext that the troops were too tired to advance, it again failed to materialize, whereupon the Field-Marshal transferred the command of all the troops in the Anafarta district to Colonel Mustapha Kemal Bey, until then commanding the 19th Division opposite Anzac, and thus laid the foundations of a triumphant career.

On the morning of the 9th Mustapha Kemal carried out the Field-Marshal's orders and succeeded in pressing us back, but it was only on the 10th, in an attack personally led by himself, that the whole ridge was definitely retaken by the Turks.

For the first time since the opening of the campaign doubts, the result of these failures, began to replace the confidence I had hitherto held of its ultimate success. It required no profound knowledge of military matters to realize the impossibility of conquering the Peninsula without further large reinforcements ; and these, I was aware, the Govern-

ment had already told the Commander-in-Chief
were not available. Withdrawal, then, seemed the
only logical alternative, unless indeed the small
amount of territory won at so heavy a cost were
clung to with the object of renewing the attack later
on.   But it was difficult to believe that such a course
would be adopted, for delay, ever favourable to the
defence, could only serve to increase the strength
of the Turkish resistance.

Nor was it merely locally that delay must prove
prejudicial to the Allies.

It had confidently been expected that success in
the Dardanelles would cause Bulgaria to abandon the
seat on the fence she had hitherto been occupying,
to come down on the side of the Entente, but the
German victories over Russia during the summer
had already gone far to influence her in the opposite
direction, and now a definite Allied defeat at Gallipoli could only have the effect of hastening her
decision to throw in her lot with the Central Powers.
Such a step must profoundly affect the Allied cause
in the Balkans, but more especially here, in the
Dardanelles.   For Turkey hitherto had been fighting
single-handed, the neutrality of Bulgaria and Roumania having effectually prevented the transit of
material assistance from Germany, from whom she
was geographically cut off; but should Bulgaria
become her ally, communications between Turkey
and Germany would immediately be established and
permit of reinforcements of artillery being thrown
into the Peninsula and render our somewhat precarious position untenable.

And yet withdrawal with all its consequences
seemed equally fatal, and when in October Sir Ian

Hamilton told the Government that he considered it unthinkable, I verily believe that he was voicing the opinion of every responsible sailor and soldier on the spot.

Only, then, by decisive victory here at the Dardanelles could either of these dangerous courses, delay or withdrawal, be averted, and yet victory seemed unattainable unless some more effective use could be made of the great latent power of the Fleet, whose heavy guns so far had proved but of small value against entrenchments and land positions.

Another attack on the Dardanelles forts on the same lines as that of March offered no more chance of success now than then, for the same adverse factors were still in operation. But to rush a squadron through the Straits was yet practicable. This plan had originally been vetoed, and justly so, for it had been reasoned that so long as the Peninsula was in hostile hands a squadron which had succeeded in forcing its way past the defences into the Marmora would find itself cut off from its base and obliged to fight its way back before it had time to accomplish any useful object. Circumstances, however, had now altered owing to the foothold we had on the Peninsula. A squadron above the Narrows now would be in a position to sever the communications of the Turkish Army which, cut off from its supplies, would thus be at the mercy of our forces.

That there were weighty objections to the Fleet undertaking such a task cannot be denied. Forts and mines, concealed batteries and torpedo-tubes constitute a defence certain of entailing heavy casualties, both in ships and men ; but ships steaming at high speed, firing heavily at stationary forts at point-blank range, veiled by smoke screens, would be no easy target ; the element of surprise would help to minimize the risks from torpedo tubes, and the means of defence against mines had been largely improved during the last few months. Losses, moreover, cannot be computed by numbers only ; they must be compared to the advantages to be gained through their means, and in this case success would be attended by advantages so great as to justify a high percentage of casualties. Boldness and surprise are strong weapons in the hands of the attackers and the more I considered the subject, the more was I impressed with the possibilities afforded by this manner of using the Fleet. Here, however, we were not in a position to judge how the Navy as a whole could afford the losses inevitable to such an enterprise, for the personnel of the ships in the Mediterranean constituted a reserve for the main Fleet and the Admiralty alone could be the arbiter in a matter of such vital importance.

I did not form these opinions suddenly ; they were the outcome of much consideration, ever gaining in strength until they eventually so materialized as to govern my conduct, when in November I suddenly and unexpectedly found myself in command of the Fleet. But operations were not at this time within the sphere of my duty nor did I consider myself justified in putting forward opinions unasked for.

The late severe fighting had, needless to say, caused a large influx of wounded into Mudros.

The hot weather and life in the trenches were also taking their toll of the health of the troops, for paratyphoid and dysentery, in neither case very severe but serious enough to cause a general lowering of

health, were very prevalent and helped to swell the
already crowded hospitals. Mudros at this time
was not a pleasant place. Flies there were in abun-
dance, in spite of the efforts of the bacteriologists
sent out from England especially to deal with them,
and a lack of shade rendered life in the town of tents
anything but agreeable, whilst fine sand penetrating
everywhere added to the general discomfort. And
yet, in spite of these drawbacks, the pervading spirit
was as high as it ever had been.

The enemy cannot have been in any better condition ; at any rate they showed no signs of activity,
and the Commander-in-Chief was enabled to send
whole battalions from the fighting line to the base
for some much-needed and hard-earned rest. Here
they were in comparative peace and quiet, an agreeable contrast to the life that many of them had been
leading for months past. These constant movements kept the small craft, of which we had now a
fairly good supply, busy and the harbour was as
full of movement and activity as ever.

"August 12. . . . Our hospitals here are ever
on the increase and to supply them with food and
water is no easy matter. Our men have now been
fighting continually since six days and must be worn
out. The weather is hot and trying and I have not
escaped a slight touch of dysentery. We shall all
be glad when the summer heat is broken. . . .
Our submarines have sunk another Turkish battleship which is always that much to the good. . . .
If the coup which we are playing now does not come
off, I cannot think what future plans will be. All
our people have done well, right from top to bottom.
The young officer I have the greatest admiration for

and certainly the Osborne-trained cadet has done credit to the place. . . . The evacuation of the wounded is a ticklish job, but up to now at any rate the Turks have fought as gentlemen and have never fired on any boats carrying wounded, though there is nothing to stop them doing so, except good feeling, because of course these boats cannot come under the Geneva Convention, having many other duties of a military nature to perform. . . . Gibson Bowles told me that the war had revealed that England's riches surpassed anything that could have been dreamed of, and he says that so long as Lloyd George is kept away from the Treasury, the country will mend itself financially in an extraordinarily short time. Alas! it will be generations before it can recoup itself in the matter of men. . . ."

The monotony of our existence was at this time pleasantly broken by a visit from Lord and Lady Brassey, who came in the *Sunbeam* to take away wounded and sick officers. It was like a breath of fresh air to see and converse with such old friends, who wore neither naval nor military uniform. An equal pleasure was the advent of another old friend, the Vicomte Emmanuel d'Harcourt, who came out in the French hospital ship the *Charles Roux*, as delegate of the French Red Cross, of which he was the Vice-President. The ship was admirably fitted out and the natural pride of all who had to do with her.

" . . . . I have seen d'Harcourt more than once. I have shown him all our hospital organization and he has shown me all over the *Charles Roux* which has all the latest inventions in surgery and such nice nurses. They are all so exactly what they should

12

be—calm, collected and business-like ; they are so universally lightly grey-haired that I am almost inclined to think that they use powder ! I cannot tell you how much I admire the general mien of the French. They are so unboastful, full of courage and determination. I often wonder what will happen to France after the war. I expect all countries will have social revolutions more or less acute. . . .

" August 15. . . . The Turks here are fighting splendidly and one regrets the fatuous policy which permitted of their joining the Germans. I hope so much that in the end they will remain in Constantinople with Bosphorus and Dardanelles internationalized. The more I think of it, the more do I believe it to be the only satisfactory solution of that question. . . .

" August 19. . . . The political atmosphere here has undergone a change since the advent to power of Venizelos, who is anxious to placate Bulgaria by giving her Kavala and hand in hand with her joining the Allies. He has a very big majority, so I suppose that anything is possible. . . . The Turkish losses have been far greater than ours and, God knows, these have been heavy enough. . . . I have just heard that our five heroes of April 25 have all got the V.C., which pleases me immensely ; late enough in all conscience, but better late than never. . . .

" August 20. . . . Fancy your having seen Mudros on the cinematograph ! And what rows that beastly cinematograph caused ! There are strict orders that none are allowed, but the French would not play up and allowed the man into their camp and amongst their men, which caused a good deal of heart-burning. The weather has become distinctly cooler, thank the Lord, and is no longer disagreeably hot. Things out here are in a very interesting state ; one's pen is held back and one's tongue tied by the fact that one never knows into whose hands letters may fall, so that of actual facts and likely possibilities one really does not dare write, and as you can imagine all one's thoughts and energies are directed in that one way. I am afraid I am getting a sort of atrophy of the brain by thinking only of one subject. Imagine to have spent six months of one's life at Lemnos ! I am indeed longing for a glimpse of the minarets of Constantinople and of the shores of the Bosphorus. Of the latter, if ever I get there, I should like to make the same use as the pashas of a century ago were supposed to do—only it would not be wives that I should drown in sacks but ——s. How sick I am getting of the politicians' ridiculous prophecies and the papers' equally ridiculous theories ! The political situation in Greece is interesting and one wonders whether Venizelos is strong enough in spite of his large majority to carry through his unpopular measures. Kavala to the Bulgarians cannot be pleasant for the Greeks, though I am one that thinks that under any circumstances Greece should not have it. Salonika is quite enough for her, and I think more than she deserves. The fact is that the more I see of them—the Greeks, I mean—the more I distrust and dislike them. . . .

" August 25. . . . Alas ! we have had to put up with much disappointment. A few days ago we were all hoping for big things, but they have not come off, though I am of opinion that they should have. . . ."

The prevailing epidemic had not passed me by, and as I had found some difficulty in shaking off its effects, the doctor strongly urged me to go away even if it were only for a couple of days. I accordingly decided to make a short visit to Athens and take the opportunity of seeing the British Minister there, with whom there were many subjects I wished to discuss. Contraband, never an easy question, in this region of mixed nationalities and lack of papers, assumed difficulties out of all proportion to its true importance, and I hoped that some of these might be overcome with his aid. There were also questions regarding the administration of the island which I hoped might be put on a more satisfactory basis, and so on August 27 I had the extreme pleasure of embarking for Athens and leaving Mudros behind me.

" August 30. . . . Mudros. . . . Here I am back again after a little jaunt to Athens, which besides having proved of some political benefit, has done me personally all the good in the world. Change of air, change of scenery, change of personnel and a few hours of comparative civilization have all helped to make another man of me, and I have returned feeling fresher and more cheerful than I have done for some little time. I went to Athens in one of the small cruisers, and had no sooner got out of the harbour than I began to feel the change. The night was glorious and we sat on deck under a full moon and felt that everything was beautiful except mankind, who was devastating the world with this damnable war. To awake in the morning and not see the eternal hospital tents and to see the beautiful Acropolis in their stead was, I felt, in itself almost enough to have justified my journey. Whom should' I run across in the hotel but—— —— upon whose neck I naturally fell and with whom I had much conversation and interchange of views. Alas ! I was not reassured. The summing up of what he told me can only be described by the word chaos. The mess the Government have made of things— supine when they should have been active and med- dlesome when they should have been quiet. I gather that at home everything is done in water- tight compartments and that no Minister has the slightest idea of what his neighbour and colleague is doing. Orders are sent out from one office un- known by another whom it indirectly affects. All this sort of muddle has, I gather, got matters into such an unravellable mess that nobody knows where they are. He,—— ——, is on a special mission sent out by the Foreign Office, and he tells me that they simply ignore him and refuse to answer his telegrams asking for instructions. He thinks it almost im- possible to bring in the Balkan States now, though three months ago it could have been done, and now it will be as much as we can do to keep them neutral. Oh ! what diplomacy ! I suppose that the Foreign Office, as usual, shuffled about and did not know their own minds and never came to any conclusions until too late. Athens is a regular hot-bed of in- trigue carried on by adventurers of all sorts and descriptions. Nobody knew I was going there, and yet I had not been an hour in the town, before two English newspaper correspondents sent me their cards and asked for an interview. I need hardly tell you that I did not see them and took steps to have it explained to them that they must be under some misapprehension because I was at Lemnos. On the afternoon of the day of my arrival Lady Cunninghame took me for a most beautiful drive towards Salamis. The joy of being once more in a motor car with nothing to remind one of Lemnos or the war! The scenery was beautiful, the air delicious and I just leaned back in the car and thought of nothing. I dined and slept with the Elliots at a villa they have taken in the country and enjoyed myself thoroughly. I drank champagne, which I had not tasted for months and months, and felt as if I were out on a real spree. . . . Our passage back to Mudros was ideal. We passed down the beautiful Gulf of Athens on an ideally beautiful afternoon, then a gorgeous sunset and a real Mediterranean night, a smooth sea and a full moon; and I arrived back here feeling quite another man and much better able to buckle to my work. . . ."

During my visit to Athens I was given plainly to understand that the Greek garrison, whose presence at Kastro had hitherto been a moral hindrance to me, would in future in no way offer any opposition to my proceedings. On my return from Athens then I hastened to pay a visit to the Greek commandant, for I now felt myself able to speak openly to him and was quite sure that he had been instructed to further all my wishes. The result was entirely satisfactory, for he told me that he would give orders to his troops, should they ever meet any British soldiers, to treat them like brothers, and that he would welcome our patrols visiting any part of the island in the performance of their duties. Thus after six months of ambiguity was the situation fairly satisfactorily cleared up.

" September 10. . . . Yesterday I went to Kastro, the capital of the island, to pay a visit to the Greek official there. Up till now I have refrained from having any communication with him and have ignored his presence. My visit to Athens, however, showed me that he had been told to put himself in my pocket, and so I went to visit him and have managed everything to my liking and several difficulties have been smoothed out. I am quite pleased with myself for the manner in which I have handled everything to do with the island, for I need hardly say that the Government have shirked all responsibility and have been of no assistance to me whatever and I have had to worry out everything for myself, which after all is perhaps as well. I have gone on the line that since they won't help me I must help myself, and have undertaken responsibilities that should have been theirs, and I have, I suppose, far outrun my instructions. Luckily, all I have done has turned up trumps, and I hope that matters are now on such a footing that even the gaucheries of the Government will not upset them. I also paid a visit to the Greek Bishop, a clever and agreeable old rogue, who I fancy uses his priest's clothing to cover a multitude of sins. Anyhow it apparently suits his book to do all that I ask him, and he is coming one day in full canonicals to consecrate a new cemetery. All this sort of thing helps to bind these people to us and makes it hard for them to work against us should they wish to. Altogether I am not displeased with my diplomacy, which has caused me to make use of that—to me—most difficult of all virtues, patience. . . . A new French Admiral has come out here to take charge of the

French base ; a charming man of the name of de
Bon, with whom I find it very easy to work. I
must say the French naval officers are very
nice. . . ."

This was the commencement of a friendship which
was to last until the Admiral's regretted death eight
years later. He eventually became Chief of the
French Naval Staff, and when I was appointed First
Sea Lord that friendship helped us to work in close
co-operation and harmony during the last eleven
months of the war and throughout the Paris peace
negotiations. A devoted servant to his country, he
was a true friend to England and his death left the
world the poorer of a true, wise and genial man.

The rapid if tardy development of Mudros gave
food for reflection on the manner in which the purely
naval attack of March had, almost unwittingly it
might be said, developed into this huge campaign
that was being fought out at such a vast expenditure
of effort, life and material. With a little foresight
on the part of those who had allowed themselves to
drift into this expedition, much of great outlay could
have been avoided. At this period anything from
150 to 200 large ships, besides a veritable cloud of
small craft, tugs, trawlers, steamboats, etc., might
at any time be counted in the anchorage. The
average number of arrivals and departures was fifty
a day, transforming the erstwhile empty harbour
into one of the busiest ports of the world. Small
wonder then at the outcry as to the amount of shipping locked up in this one expedition when ships
were becoming scarce and their services in greater
request. But an amphibious campaign such as this,
where the fighting line was separated from its base

by 60, and from England by nearly 3,000 miles of sea, could not be conducted without the employment of ships badly needed for other purposes. Nor from the very nature of the circumstances could they be employed economically. Coaling difficulties, causing the leviathans in use for the transport of troops to be delayed in their return; lack of facilities, rendering the process of unloading the store-ships a slow one; activity of enemy submarines, entailing frequent delays in sailing; all these reasons combined to swell the number of vessels required.

"September 14. . . . I wish I could explain to you how this place is expanding. In the last three weeks there has practically arisen a new town of about 10,000 inhabitants. Every hut and every bit of provisions has had to be landed from the store-ships, for which purpose three big piers and several smaller ones have been built. A big plant for distilling water has been erected; drainage undertaken, etc. We have hundreds of Egyptian labourers and employ a good many Greeks as well, and you will be amused to hear that I have set up a labour bureau and am negotiating for a bank. The French are rather in a state of mind because their paper money has so depreciated. The English paper pound notes are at a premium, thank goodness. Bolstering up French credit is not an easy task, but I am trying to do it, though hardly expect to succeed. . . . I think you will find me a much more patient being than I used to be. Certainly I have had to practise that virtue here. Many of its fruits are now ripening, and things that some time ago I hardly dared believe would come off are actually in existence. I have had a good deal of quiet opposition to meet, but I have met it with similar weapons and am now getting all I wanted.

"September 17. . . . My banking scheme is, I think, going to turn up trumps after all, and if it does and I get one going the difficulty about the French money should be much eased. The French are suffering somewhat from visits of Senators and Deputies; however, they don't seem to pay any attention to them really. One French Admiral told me only to-day that he felt pretty confident that there would be an end of parliamentary government after the war though he had no idea of what was likely to take its place. 'Sufficient unto the day, etc.'"

The banking scheme materialized and a branch of the Banque d'Athènes was opened in the village under joint English and French auspices. It greatly improved the financial position of the Allied forces, since all illegitimate attempts on the part of Greek *mercantès* to depreciate British and French money were thereby frustrated. The rate of exchange was regulated by a daily bulletin received from the National Bank of Greece and all bills of exchange and other monetary transactions were henceforth negotiated at the current rates. Local merchants also benefited by the institution as they were no longer dependent upon casual opportunities for the conveying of specie. The peasants, however, were for a long time more trustful of their stockings than of the till of the bank, and it was estimated that there can have been little short of £30,000 hoarded in the island, whereas eight months before there had probably been less than 50,000 drachmas.

The large agglomeration of humanity extraneous to the island that had been brought together in such a comparatively small space under conditions so abnormal required other schemes besides that of banking for the regulation of its affairs and the maintenance of order. Since one part only was subject to martial law and the other not, the steps that I had to take were necessarily arbitrary. A strict censorship both at Mudros and Kastro and a surveillance of the passengers using the latter port were established, the former under the able direction of Commander Cotterell, R.N.V.R., who had already rendered good service in laying cables, and that more than once under fire, the latter under the management of Mr. McLaughlan, a Scotchman by birth and a landowner in Cyprus, where he had had some previous experience in the police. He organized a small native plain-clothes police force and intelligence department by whose means I was kept well informed of all that went on in the island. Stringent measures were adopted to restrain the sale of liquor to the troops, and somewhat to my astonishment the publicans and mayors of the various villages not only acquiesced in them but put no obstacles in the way of their being carried out—in all cases except that of one liquor shop whose real owner I eventually discovered was no less a person than my friend the Bishop ! Compensation for damage done and for land occupied by the troops was settled by a court that I set up consisting of two British officers and two Greek mayors, presided over by the Government Secretary. The claims put forward were generally exorbitant, but the decisions were fair and in spite of drastic reduction well received by the people concerned, who were not wanting in commercial acumen.

In one case I could have wished that there existed a local law for the compulsory sale of land. An old lady flatly refused to sell a small piece of ground required for enlarging the cemetery, except for a sum representing about £300 an acre. She held out for this exaggerated price in spite of the entreaties of her numerous family, who doubtless thought that British gold—or rather notes—would prove easier of division at her demise than a plot of almost worthless ground. After arbitration a reasonable sum was offered, but the importunate widow remained adamant, and for all I know is so still, for when I left the island the land was in our possession and the proffered money lodged in the bank.

Busy as all these occupations kept me, I found time at the end of this month to pay an eagerly looked forward visit to Anzac, where a warm welcome awaited me from General Birdwood. It is difficult to describe the impression stamped on my mind during the two days I spent in that place, so unique in its situation, its surroundings, and its circumstances. The now famous " Brighton Beach," only some 30 or 40 yards in breadth, lay at the foot of the steep cliff at the top of which were situated our trenches. It swarmed with half-naked men whose skins had been burnt a deep mahogany, unloading lighters and carrying their contents of provisions, stores and ammunition from the wooden piers up the cliff side. Occasionally would be heard the discharge of a gun and a shell would fall harmlessly into the sea crowded with men bathing, who took not the slightest notice of these demonstrations unless it were to jeer at their futility. There were, however, danger zones known and avoided by all, but unnoticeable to the uninitiated. The whole of the cliff side was honeycombed with dug-outs and from the unceasing flow of men over its face, produced the idea of a vast ant-heap.

The General's quarters were situated a short way up the cliff and consisted of a dug-out with a wattle for its outer wall. The dimensions were such that when he and I were there together there was hardly room for anybody else. It served as bedroom, dining-room and office, while his bathroom was the sea. It was approached by what must once have been a goat-track, but had now from frequent use become a fairly negotiable path, leading eventually to that curious underground labyrinth of passages, the trenches. A long day going the rounds disagreeably reminded me that my sedentary life of the last six months was not conducive to physical fitness, and I followed the active and energetic General with an intense interest, gradually changing into an ardent desire to hide from my companions the leg-weariness that came over me. Never was I more pleased than when I found myself once more in his dug-out, hot and tired, but thrilled with all I had seen. I shall never forget one Australian sniper whose features clearly denoted an admixture of Mongol blood. The man was perched in his camouflaged look-out station—motionless of eye or limb even when I addressed him except for an occasional almost involuntary movement of his fingers round the trigger of his rifle. He told me he was watching the head of a Turk only a few yards distant—quite invisible to me, look as I might—and that he was only awaiting the moment when the head should look up to send a bullet through it. He had beside him a rough stick full of notches, each one of which he laconically informed me represented " an addition to his bag."

I left Anzac with regret, for the pervading spirit of confidence was so exhilarating as to leave a deep impression upon me.

A destroyer took me on to Suvla, where I met an old friend in General Byng, who kindly showed me all that was of interest and explained the relative position of his own and the enemy's forces. Like Anzac there were zones that were never free from annoyance from the enemy's guns, but unlike Anzac there was not that air of ancient tradition that the five months' occupation had imparted to the former place. General Byng had only taken up his command on August 24, and was still impressed by the difference between warfare in France and warfare in the Gallipoli Peninsula. Here too I once more saw Commander Unwin, who had been in command of the lighters on the occasion of the Suvla landing and was now with undiminished energy and success conducting affairs on the beach. A line of nets enclosed the bay, rendering it safe from submarine attack, and here were anchored two battleships, the *Venerable* and the *Glory*, ready to open fire on the enemy should he give them an opportunity. I returned to Mudros all the better for a glimpse of trench warfare and life on the beaches that gave me a practical idea of its troubles and difficulties.

The results of the failure of our last attacks were not long in making themselves felt, whilst in another theatre of the war events were occurring that were seriously to affect the outcome of our struggle. The Austro-German invasion of Servia, made possible by the collapse of Russia in the summer, finally convinced Bulgaria, now persuaded of the impossibility of an Allied victory in the Dardanelles, of the invincibility of the Central Powers. She mobilized and joined in the onslaught on her old foe and neighbour. The Servian debâcle cleared the way for the enemy to Salonika, the capture of which would compromise our position in the Mediterranean to an even greater extent than the opening of communications between Turkey and Germany that could not but imperil before long our forces on the Peninsula. Greece promptly mobilized and it was hoped that she intended fulfilling her treaty obligations towards Servia. Rumours, however, of a secret understanding between her and Germany had for a long time been current, and their truth seemed to be borne out by her failure to come to Servia's assistance. Venizelos resigned on October 6 and the political outlook became darker than ever.

To me this resignation came as a personal misfortune, for under his tenure of office my position in Lemnos, though always ambiguous, had been comparatively easy and I did not know how his successor would view the situation. Fortunately, however, any chance of hindrance to my projects was diminished by the removal of the Greek garrison on their mobilization.

The danger at Salonika was very real and very close. The nearest Allied troops were those on the Peninsula and on October 1 we began to be inundated with telegrams which clearly showed the intention of the War Council to use part of them in that sphere. After many orders and counter-orders definite instructions were received for one English and one

French division to be sent there, and the transports conveying the last detachments sailed on October 8.

" September 27. . . . Bulgaria's sudden mobilization seems to have come as a shock to most people. I cannot understand why, for though I hoped matters would not take this turn it did not in the least surprise me. The Greeks are supposed to be very keen to have it out with Bulgaria, though I fancy they do not relish the idea of other possible enemies. Our information, for what it is worth, tells us that the Bulgarian Army will fight Servia or Greece, but never Russia or England. The Greek mobilization came as a surprise to me, for I had been led to believe that in spite of Venizelos she would not do so, but the whole matter has been one of bungling, underhand and dishonest diplomacy on both sides. Nobody has any clear vision and so anything may happen. It is difficult to imagine that two hostile armies can face each other for any length of time without coming to blows, especially with so much behind to egg them on. . . .

" October 4. . . . I saw d'Harcourt to-day for a few minutes. He has just returned from Salonika and tells me that the German element there is very strong. He also told me he had known Ferdinand (of Bulgaria) intimately all his life and had not one single good word to say for him. . . .

" October 7. . . . We have been kept on the tiptoe of excitement and suspense here during the last three days. Contradictory telegrams of every sort and kind pouring in which does not give one a very good idea of what is going on at home and does not improve the impression I have of those that are placed in authority over us. Present indications go to show that Bulgaria has definitely thrown in her lot with the enemy, and indeed one cannot be greatly surprised, for how anybody could desire England with her wobblers who call themselves statesmen for an ally passes comprehension. . . . How we are suffering from spurious democracy ! When will people realize that human beings are human beings, and could not, even if they wished to, which they do not, inhabit Utopia ? . . . I often go about and talk to the sick troops and you can't think how nice they are. It is amazing to think that with such splendid material the country should have gone so far towards the dogs. It makes me mad when I hear people praising Lloyd George ; do they ever consider that we are reaping as he has sown ? Truly we are a remarkable people and it is wonderful how, out here, we feel the effects of our indiscipline. However I have given myself pretty strong authority and have ignored both the law of the land and the King's regulations and Admiralty instructions. Luckily that sort of responsibility does not lie heavily on me, but I resent the half-hearted measures of the Admiralty and their trembling at responsibility. . . ."

The Government had just succeeded in making my position more equivocal than it already was by their recent refusal to extend the scope of my authority by putting the place under martial law. Some of the crews of the many merchant ships passing through Mudros were inclined to give trouble and I had no legal powers to deal with them summarily. I got over the difficulty by considering Mudros as being in a war-zone, though whether that entitled me to punish want of discipline as I did I very much

13

doubt. Amongst many similar cases was one of a crew that refused to continue the work of unloading after 6 p.m. on the pretext that it was against their trades-union rules ! After vainly pointing out that the enemy did not recognize their rules and comparing their circumstances to those of their fellow-countrymen in the trenches and reproaching them with the unpatriotic nature of their behaviour, I had sentenced them to a term of cells when one of their number protested that he was a Russian subject ; but upon his being told that in this case he would be sent on board the Russian cruiser *Askold*, then in the harbour, he begged that he might rather undergo his punishment, for he felt sure that once on board the Russian ship he would be hung at the yardarm !

" October 9, 1915. . . . We have been living in a perfect whirl of diplomatic excitement during the last few days and the telegrams received only emphasize the fact of the watertight-compartment working of the various Ministries at home. The attitude of Bulgaria is still a puzzle—there is only one thing certain, and that is that she wants Macedonia.

" October 12. . . . Who should unexpectedly turn up here yesterday but O'Beirne on his way to Athens from Sofia. He came to luncheon with me, but was not as interesting as I had hoped. He is evidently Bulgarophile, at any rate Grecophobe, in which latter I am heartily with him. He, too, says that the Tsar (Ferdinand) will find considerable difficulty in getting the army to fight either against Russians or English. He says his three months' residence in Sofia was not long enough for him to get a true insight into the Bulgarian character and

altogether did not seem, I thought, very sure of himself. He and his French colleague left the country
with every sort of honour, Ferdinand assuring them
that it was with the greatest regret that he saw them
go and that he (F.) could not for the life of him
understand why the Allies had broken off relations
with Bulgaria ! ! . . . The Greek mobilization continues, but I am sure they have no intention of fighting if they can possibly help it, and even if they
should come in on our side they would now, I think,
prove a great deal more trouble than they are
worth. . . .

" October 16. . . . The situation here gets more
muddled every day. Russia is at war with Bulgaria,
but apparently we and the French are not, and yet
we both of us have troops at Salonika. I believe
the Government hug to themselves the notion that
they are making a demonstration—a demonstration
of 15,000 or 18,000 men in these days of hundreds
of thousands and millions. It would be ludicrous
were it not so pitiful. I have just heard that Hamilton is going. With a new man who knows what may
happen ? . . ."

CHAPTER IX

SOME little time elapsed before I became fully acquainted with the circumstances attending Sir Ian Hamilton's recall, and I wondered whether change of command foreboded change of policy. Time was slipping away. If some definite decision were not quickly arrived at, winter gales might well preclude any possibility either of renewing the attack, or of withdrawing from the Peninsula.

I was well aware of the late Commander-in-Chief's sentiments : withdrawal, he had proclaimed unthinkable ; but no one could guess the opinions of his successor, Sir Charles Monro. Coming straight from the command of an army in France, I feared that he might be of the " Western " school of thought, i.e., one of those who looked upon the Dardanelles campaign as a " side-show," diverting troops from the only theatre of the war where a decision could be obtained. If this should be the case, the War-Council, I argued, had probably decided to abandon the campaign, and the diversion to Salonika of two divisions of our dwindling force seemed to strengthen this view.

Salonika was occupying our thoughts and attention almost as much as did the Peninsula, for the presence of Allied troops considerably increased our naval commitments. The Gulf had to be protected with a net-defence, new cables laid and our patrols extended. The enemy, needless to say, had to be kept out of Salonika ; but Greece, who had invoked our aid and whose primary duty it was to defend her own territory, was taking no steps to protect the disembarkation of her own and Allied troops now being rushed into the town.

" October 18, 1915. . . . War actually declared with Bulgaria, and Greece still playing with us and trying to make us pull her chestnuts out of the fire. What irritates me so, is the fact that the Greek Government's sympathies are so evidently pro-German. I believe the only honest and wise course now would be to send her an ultimatum, telling her that unless she threw in her lot with ours and honestly helped us, we should take such steps as we deemed necessary for our own good. She has quite deserved such treatment, for she has wheedled us on with false hopes. They are a beastly nation and the Foreign Office are fools. We are all absolutely in the dark as to policy at Salonika, and naturally so, because I feel quite certain that there is none.

" . . . October 21, 1915. Trafalgar Day, and here we are, hobnobbing with our excellent friends, the French, while together we concert measures for the destruction of Germans ; so runs the world and the whirligig of time brings strange changes. . . . You will be interested to hear that the Bank is a great success and has quite paralyzed the illegitimate efforts of the Greeks to depreciate French and British money. After all, even Lemnos can be amusing sometimes. . . . The French and Greeks are pouring troops into Salonika and I wonder how the muddle will end ; I should never be surprised to find the Greeks arrayed against us. I should have enormous pleasure in hoisting the Union Jack in the island and it would serve the Greeks right if they lost it.

" . . . October 22, 1915. . . . The weather has just broken and to-day we have real rain, the first for many months. Dunraven has come in in his yacht for wounded officers; I dined with him last night and thoroughly enjoyed the change. I have been looking at a picture of Ferdinand in one of the illustrated papers—a horrid countenance. I wonder that all these countries do not get rid of their imported monarchs. How can they be anything but self-seeking; how on earth can a German be a Bulgarian, or a Dane a Greek? They should be deported to some Pacific island and allowed to intrigue among the natives."

It was at this time that Commodore Keyes, the Vice-Admiral's Chief of the Staff, came to tell me he was proceeding to England with his (the Vice-Admiral's) consent to lay before the Admiralty and the War Council a plan for rushing a squadron through the Straits. He asked me whether he could state that it met with my approval, and this I authorized him to do, coinciding as it did, in principle at any rate, with my hopes and views. I asked what the Vice-Admiral thought of it and was told that he did not regard the scheme favourably, but that he had raised no objection to Keyes putting it forward and urging its adoption. I was delighted with the turn taken by events and greatly impressed by de Robeck's broad-mindedness in allowing his Chief of the Staff to press forward a scheme in whose efficacy he had but little belief.

Keyes departed on October 23, taking with him my most cordial wishes for success, and I was left wondering how matters would shape themselves. If Keyes' mission should prove successful, what line would de Robeck take? If unsuccessful, how would it fare with him and with me? I had, however, but little time for vain speculation and was content to await events.

The summer weather had broken and we began to have more of those gales that multiplied our difficulties and delayed communication, serving as a warning of what might be expected in the winter. When would the War-Council make up their mind?

" October 26, 1915. . . . Events on the Servian front are occupying everybody's attention and interest, but we are kept very badly informed of the happenings there. The whole thing is so complicated, but I think that it is Greece that is the villain of the piece. I should not wonder a bit if there were a secret treaty or arrangement between her and Germany, the latter probably guaranteeing the former immune from Bulgarian attack on condition that she does not help Servia; that seems to me the most likely reason for her otherwise almost inexplicable conduct. It is so obvious that our Government have no policy, no plans, no strategy and are merely drifting. . . . Telegrams last night to say the Servians have checked the German attack and that the French have fallen upon the Bulgarians. These beastly telegrams one always knows to be unreliable, and yet one cannot help believing that the optimistic ones are true. . . . We are always at high pressure here, always something unexpected turning up and are never able to get beyond our work. It comes from the policy of drift at home and not knowing what they are after; we are only able to go on from day to day and really it is lucky we can even do that. . . ."

The new Commander-in-Chief arrived on the 27th of this month, during a gale of wind that must have given him an early practical exhibition of the difficulties attending an amphibious campaign. It was the Vice-Admiral whom the change of command would mostly affect ; his relations with the Commander-in-Chief were almost daily, my duties hardly brought me into contact with him. A change which affected me more personally was caused by the promotion of Contre-Amiral Guépratte, the gallant French Admiral who, from the very commencement, had been our cordial and enthusiastic collaborator.

" October 28, 1915. . . . I was invited to a farewell luncheon to-day by Guépratte, whom we all like so much. He embraced me on both cheeks in front of all the officers of his ship and of the guard drawn up on deck to do me honour. That sort of thing, however, no longer has any terrors for me, so that I was able to return his embrace without any signs of confusion. I also did quite well in an impromptu speech in French, for which I was in no ways prepared, because the *déjeuner* was not a big affair and it never entered my head there would be any speechifying. . . . The last six months have been a great trial to my patience. You cannot think how trying I sometimes find the people who cannot and will not recognize the limitations of others, sailors of soldiers and soldiers of sailors. One has to keep a cheerful countenance and smooth away small difficulties, so small that one would have thought they required no smoothing at all. Big difficulties do not seem to affect me in the same manner—it is the little stupidities that I find so trying. I try to be as impartial as a Solomon, and if I succeed, then I must say that the soldiers are worse than the sailors and the doctors worst of all —doctors of both services. . . . I think I can understand the neutrals—real neutrals—being alarmed at the possibilities that a defeat of the Central Powers might bring about, for the only chance in favour of law and order after a victory of the Allies rests in the fact that men and women who have gone through the experiences of the war must emerge from it with very different ideas. Can you imagine the average English Radical who has served in France or out here returning to vote for Lloyd George and Co.? I should think they would set up a dictator rather than do that. I don't know whether the world in general will be any better for the war; but if so, I am afraid it will be so much in the far future that neither you nor I will be alive to reap the benefits. . . ."

Accounts of the state of affairs prevailing at Salonika were such as to cause some anxiety. I therefore determined to see with my own eyes what was going on and render any assistance I could.

" November 4th, 1915. . . . I have just returned from a two days' visit to Salonika. I have brought back with me a very unpleasant impression, I am sorry to say. We have no one there with credentials to deal with the Greeks, and as a natural result chaos reigns. I sent a telegram to the Admiralty on the subject dealing with even the diplomatic and political side of the business. I hesitated some time before doing so, wondering whether, if I went too far, I might not spoil the game by making them think I was

digging in ground that was not my own. However,
after weighing the pros and cons I let it go, and
erased nothing. Anyhow they will have heard the
truth. Salonika swarms with Jews and Germans
and their agents go about nakedly and unashamed,
knowing full well that we have nothing on our side
to counter them. It is too melancholy for words.
Every Greek is fully convinced that the Germans
are going to win, and since they naturally think of
nothing but themselves they are loth to attach themselves to what they believe will be the under-dog.
They are, as a nation, quite incapable of seeing
further than Athens or Salonika, and fear of the
near future makes them incapable of judging of
anything further ahead. I am inclined to believe
the story that Greece has a secret understanding
with Germany whereby she is guaranteed from
Bulgarian attack provided she does not help Servia ;
but what about the squabble for Salonika afterwards ? I cannot believe that anything less than a
promise of it has persuaded Bulgaria to join in.
What a mess ! Can anybody be surprised that such
neutrals as are left look askance at us when they see
the way in which we conduct our business. As I
write I hear of the fall of the Greek Government,
which I can only imagine heralds the return of
Venizelos—but it is too late, and those wretched
Servians, betrayed and befooled, can only be wiped
out of existence or have to surrender *en bloc* ;
if all the accounts one hears at Salonika are true I
don't see that anything else can happen. I am itch-
ing to get back there and run the show, but I see
little chance of their letting me away from here.
This spot must always remain the centre, unless

there comes some very radical change, which at present I do not foresee. . . . Well, the Navy has been our salvation so far, though it has not played a very showy part. . . . Salonika was an extraordinary sight ; the quays and principal streets European, all behind them quite Oriental, Jews in strange costumes rubbing shoulders with baggy-trousered Balkanese (I refuse to believe they are all Greeks), British, French and Greek officers and soldiers vigorously saluting each other in the streets —German agents looking contemptuously on—motor cars, overloaded donkeys, and all the mixed rabble of a Levantine town forming an interesting kaleidoscope. Huge British transports lying alongside the quays, the back streets blocked by Greek soldiers leading their sturdy little transport ponies and donkeys ; a curious medley of East and West, of war and peace, and as a final contrast new Greek churches facing old Turkish mosques and minarets. I had an hour or two to spare one afternoon, which I spent in driving out in a motor car to see the camps in a wonderful plain outside the town that rather reminded me of the Roman Campagna. . . . I am sorry to say that we have evidences of German brutalities out here. A boatload of wretched undefended people from a torpedoed ship was picked up at sea with everybody in it shot by rifles. I cannot imagine the state of mind that makes it possible for any one to commit such deeds ; not as in the passion of battle—but in cold blood ! It is horrible and I don't like to let my mind dwell upon it. . . . You will be amused to hear that some of my energies are now being directed towards some attempt to get back into British hands some of the hard cash that the natives here have quite honestly obtained from us and are hoarding in their stockings. I am trying to get them to trade with Cyprus and Malta in fruit, vegetables, and such like healthy commodities for the troops. The Bank tells us there must be £30,000 of English money hoarded away in the island. Fancy what a triumph that would be if I could get that into circulation again and into British hands. ..."

On my return from Salonika I learnt without surprise that Sir Charles Monro had already reported unfavourably on the military situation and had strongly recommended the immediate evacuation of the Peninsula. In his telegram of October 31st he gave full and weighty reasons for arriving at this conclusion. After setting forth the technical military disadvantages from which we were suffering, of which I, as a naval officer, could have no authoritative opinion, he went on to say that " the beaches and piers on which they were dependent for all requirements in personnel and material were exposed to registered and observed artillery fire " and that " the communications were insecure and dependent on the weather." Never since April 25 had we done anything else than labour under these disadvantages, and yet for seven months we had clung to the positions gained and had on more than one occasion been within an ace of final success, the failure to attain it having been primarily due—as all military opinion agrees—to an insufficiency of shells. The deterioration of the health of the troops that had helped to influence Sir Charles' views was in a great measure due to the hot weather now past, and to some extent perhaps to the inaction to which they had been condemned for the last ten weeks. Their morale, however, had never been undermined and a new offensive would, I believe, even now have had an electrifying effect upon the whole force. I fully recognized that the time was now nearly past when another military attack was feasible, for every day of delay was increasing the difficulties which were weighing with Sir Charles, but in my opinion it was even now not too late to retrieve the situation by pushing a squadron through the Narrows so long as our troops held their present positions and were able to profit by the advantages that such a move must necessarily give them. It is certain that the drawbacks entailed by climatic conditions and sickness must have been equally shared by the enemy, as proved by their lack of initiative since the battles of August—though now, no doubt, they were awaiting the time when, owing to Bulgaria having joined the Central Powers, communications between Germany and Turkey would be established and allow of Teutonic artillery and munitions being poured into the Peninsula. All the more reason, therefore, for us to act promptly before they could thus be reinforced.

Surprise has been expressed that considering the near approach of winter with its accompanying gales the War Council did not put Sir Charles' recommendations for evacuation into effect, but it must not be forgotten that Commodore Keyes was at this time personally urging, as I knew he could urge, that the Navy should be allowed to make a last attempt to snatch at victory.

For the first time I welcomed the indecisions of the War Council, discerning in them, as I believed, promise of the fulfilment of our hopes.

Generals Birdwood, Byng and Davies were all in agreement with the Commander-in-Chief's tactical views, though the first made strong reservations with regard to the political and strategic effects that the retirement would, in his opinion, produce in the East; but before the War Council could be induced to authorize a step they so evidently dreaded even weightier opinion was to be taken, for Lord Kitchener announced his intention of coming out to judge for himself how matters stood.

Lord Kitchener was in principle adverse to abandonment of the campaign, chiefly on account of its consequences to Egypt, and in a telegram of November 3 to General Birdwood announcing his early arrival at Mudros, told him he believed the Admiralty would agree to a naval attempt to force the Straits, and bade him carefully explore all means of military co-operation, adding " there will probably be a change in naval command, Wemyss being appointed in command to carry through the naval part of the work," and ending up with the significant sentences : " I absolutely refuse to sign orders for evacuation, which I think would be the gravest disaster and would condemn a large percentage of our men to death or imprisonment. Monro will be appointed to the command of the Salonika force."

Here then is evidence that up to this date, November 3, the naval project was still being favourably considered, for the War Council had gone so far as to contemplate changes of command, replacing officers known to be opposed to the naval scheme by others advocating its adoption.

But changes of mind were as sudden as they were frequent, and on the very next day, November 4,

Lord Kitchener informed General Birdwood that a renewal of the naval attack might not be approved, directing him secretly and quietly to work out a scheme for getting the troops off the Peninsula.

It may be expedient here to explain that at the time I had no knowledge of the contents—or even the existence—of this telegraphic correspondence between Lord Kitchener and the Generals. My position was a delicate one, due to serving under an Admiral who, temporarily my senior, was substantively my junior officer, and was not rendered any less so by the difference of opinion existing between us on the all-important question of naval action. Under ordinary circumstances any such difference would have been no consequence, for as already stated, operations lay beyond the scope of my duties; but in this case my views had been sought not by the Vice-Admiral but by his Chief of the Staff. Although the whole matter was perfectly aboveboard and Admiral de Robeck aware of all that had taken place, he had never broached the subject to me and I therefore felt it impossible to advert to it. The awkwardness of the situation arose from the practical certainty that if the plan were to be adopted, Admiral de Robeck would not remain in command to carry it out and from the probability that I should be selected to succeed him. It was therefore not sufficient that there should be no intrigue, there must be no suspicion of intrigue, and though persuaded that no such thought would enter Admiral de Robeck's mind, fears that suspicions might be aroused in the Fleet and create a division of opinion, constrained me to silence.

Lord Kitchener, accompanied by Sir Henty Mc-

Mahon, the High Commissioner, and Sir John Maxwell, the General commanding the troops in Egypt, arrived at Mudros on November 9 and took up his quarters on board the *Lord Nelson*. The following days were spent in general inspection of troops and positions on the Peninsula and in conferences. He had early proof of our difficulties of communication when on summoning his Generals it was blowing too hard to admit of their coming over from the Peninsula, and the Field-Marshal's astonishment that his orders could not be obeyed found expression in the surprised exclamation : " And this is what they call war ! "

From the outset it was clear that in his eyes the campaign derived its chief importance from the immunity from invasion it afforded to Egypt, and when convinced of the military necessity of withdrawing the troops from the Peninsula he sought a means of using them to effect the same object by proposing to land them at Ayas Bay, close to Alexandretta, to cut the Turkish railway communications with the East and South. Whatever the strategic advantages of such a move, the practical difficulties in now carrying it out would have proved well-nigh insuperable. Ayas Bay is an almost open anchorage sheltered only from the North and East—difficult of defence and offering every disadvantage from a naval point of view. There was no convenient base nearer than Alexandria and the transference of the whole of the administrative machinery from Mudros, besides the transference of all the small craft, lighters and material, would have been a task of great magnitude and difficulty, occupying time that could ill be afforded. I set forth all the drawbacks, and was much relieved when the project was vetoed from England.

The net result of the conferences was that on November 22, nearly a fortnight after his arrival on the scene, Lord Kitchener telegraphed his recommendations that Suvla and Anzac should be immediately evacuated and Helles retained. Of the retention of Helles I never could see the object. The tactical reasons rendering advisable the evacuation of Suvla and Anzac applied in an equal degree to Helles, for once a retirement was commenced it seemed highly improbable that any further operations would be undertaken.

I had more than one long conversation with Lord Kitchener. He had met Commodore Keyes in London, but did not tell me what passed between them. Unaware as I was then that my name had been mentioned as a likely successor to Admiral de Robeck in an eventual naval attack, I did not mention the subject to him, as otherwise I would have done and as I did later on to Sir Charles Monro. Greece was the principal topic of our talk, and I related to him all the difficulties I had encountered and the dangers I apprehended. These, of course, must have been as clear to him as they were to me ; a repetition of them, however, by the man on the spot might, I hoped, do some good. He spoke of his impending visit to King Constantine at Athens, a visit that he told me he was making against his judgment at the strong instance of our Government. I never subsequently had an opportunity of hearing from him what occurred at this interview, of which no tangible results ever appeared.

On November 22 came to an end Lord Kitchener's

14

memorable visit to Mudros, which, notwithstanding
the gravity of the situation and the importance of
the decisions it had witnessed, was not without its
lighter incidents. The Field-Marshal for some reason
not elucidated, but said by scoffers to be distrust
of his colleagues in the Cabinet, had brought with
him his seal of office. On one occasion, on leaving
the ship he inadvertently left it lying about in
his cabin, where it was found by his bluejacket
orderly, who recognizing an article of rarity and value
brought it to the Captain, who to his astonishment thus found himself invested with the seals of
office.

With Lord Kitchener's departure we realized that
a crisis had been reached when definite action one
way or another could no longer be postponed, and
whilst impatiently awaiting the Government's orders,
resumed the tenour of our ways.

"November 21. . . . I am having an amusing
passage of arms with the Greek Bishop, who is a
real old scoundrel. The only thing he thinks of is
money, and I have just discovered that he is the
real owner of a horrible little inn that sells appalling
spirits to the troops. It is some way off in the
country and difficult to deal with, and I have had
to shut it down altogether; and now in his rage
and disappointment the Bishop has, by a slip of
the tongue, actually owned up to being the proprietor.
In the meantime he is trying to bribe me with pre-
sents of partridges and honey, but I retaliate by
sending him the equivalent value in port wine.
His latest move had been to act as *agent provocateur*
between me and the French, but my friend, the French
General, is quite wide awake and having had some

previous experience of Greek Orthodox bishops, sent him away with a flea in his ear. As he has been trying to bribe me he is quite quelled for the present, and has the mortification of knowing that whilst outwardly I keep up the semblances of friendship I am thoroughly acquainted with his methods. He is now crying misery and trying to make out that ' his flock ' is so poor, but I happen to know through the Bank that there is not far short of £40,000 more in the island now than when we came here nine months ago. I am beginning to think that German gold is finding its way into his pockets.

" I have been carefully reading Mr. Asquith's statement of November 2 in the House. I cannot glean much comfort from it. A Committee of the Cabinet can never succeed. So long as there are twenty-one people holding Cabinet rank, every one of them must bear his portion of responsibility, and how can they do this when they have an inner Cabinet of five or seven members who consult in private and act without their knowledge ? It is ridiculous and can only lead to worse confusion than before. Personally I think that the Cabinet should consist of Prime Minister, Chancellor of the Exchequer, Secretaries for War and Foreign Affairs and First Lord of the Admiralty, with perhaps the addition of two more men who should be chosen for their personal qualifications quite irrespective of the posts they hold. . . . I heard a very extraordinary story a few days ago from the lips of the man who was Medical Director-General of the Navy at the time. It seems that in the autumn and winter of 1913 it was suddenly discovered that there was a ring of Germans who were attempting to buy up and corner all the medical stores in England, and it was only by this man's initiative in taking steps on his own account to buy them all for the Services that it was stopped. There was no single firm of manufacturers of these goods in England that had not been approached and were on the point of selling. . . .

"November 24. . . . I spent two hours to-day in a sort of diplomatic and wordy warfare with my friend the Greek Bishop, who, I am glad to say, was routed at all points. I insisted on having another Greek in the cabin as a witness, besides the Government Secretary. By the warm manner he shook my hand on departure I knew how mortified he was by his failure. So I suppose I must be ready for more underhand attacks, but I feel quite able to cope with him. The fact is that the natives, after a trial of both, prefer Turkish rule to Greek, and English to either, so I am in the lucky position of having popular feeling on my side. . . ."

Lord Kitchener's departure coincided with the return from England of Commodore Keyes, who immediately came to see me to relate his experiences. He had laid the plan drawn up by the Vice-Admiral's Staff before both the War Council and the Admiralty, and although it had never received any direct acquiescence he had left England with the sincere conviction that it was favourably regarded by both those bodies as well as by Lord Kitchener, with whom he had had an interview before the latter's departure for Mudros. The French Admiralty, he also told me, regarded the proposal with favour and would help. These quick changes and hesitancies were baffling but, what did seem clear was that, should the Fleet make the attempt to push through the Straits, it would not be under Admiral de Robeck's command but under mine. The expectation that after all we should get our way, appeared therefore almost confirmed when two days later, on the evening of November 24, the Commodore came on board to inform me that the Vice-Admiral was departing for England the next morning on leave. I went to see him before he left, but no mention was made of the matter uppermost in both our minds, and I assumed command in a state of uncertainty as to whether my tenure was temporary or not.

CHAPTER X

FINDING myself thus placed in command under such unusual circumstances; led to believe by the course of events that de Robeck's return was by no means certain, I had quickly to make up my mind whether I could regard my position as temporary or permanent, for my action would in one case differ very considerably from my conduct in the other. If I were merely de Robeck's locum tenens, it would be my duty to follow his policy—if not, to pursue my own. After grave consideration, in which pressure of time was the dominating factor, I decided on the latter course. From that moment I never ceased advocating with all the strength in my possession the action which since the reverses of August I had been pondering and hoping to see carried out. I had an able and enthusiastic collaborator in Commodore Keyes, who remained on as Chief of the Staff and who had always been of the same opinion as myself. We spent many hours together elaborating a series of telegrams to the Admiralty urging an immediate naval attack and putting forward every argument in its favour. In this we had the invaluable assistance of Captain Godfrey, R.M.A., who saw, as we saw, that in our proposals lay the only chance of saving the situation.

I lost no time in seeing Sir Charles Monro, from whom I hid nothing. I explained to him the position in which I was placed, expounded my policy, and told him I meant to push it to the utmost of my power. I pointed out how gravely I viewed the difficulties of evacuation ; how, from a purely naval point of view, it might, at this season of the year, result in a great disaster ; and after expressing to the best of my ability my conviction that the Navy could, by the proposed action, materially assist the Army to overcome its difficulties, and even be the means of changing defeat into victory, asked him two specific questions : What would be the effect on the military situation on the Peninsula if a squadron of battleships succeeded in forcing the Straits and getting beyond the Narrows ? and, if such an operation were undertaken, whether it would be better, from a military point of view, for the Army to make an attack simultaneously or after the squadron had got through ?

Immediately after my interview and before receiving the answers which he was to give me in writing, I informed the Admiralty of what I was doing and earnestly asked that definite orders for evacuation might not be issued until I had had further consultations with the Commander-in-Chief and time to send them my appreciation of the situation.

I shifted my flag from the *Europa* to the *Lord Nelson*, and, critical though the situation was, I found the change in the character of my duties was exhilarating, the only drawback being the circumstances under which de Robeck, with whom I had throughout worked so cordially and from whom I had received so much consideration, had left. I like to think that the difference of our opinions never clouded a friendship of so many years' standing.

I felt sure that General Monro had but little faith

in the capability of our plans to turn the tide, and I
awaited his answer with some misgiving. And now,
just when we felt the want of some encouragement,
just when a little good luck might have turned the
balance in our favour, fate dealt us a blow which
I feared would only stiffen his resistance. On November 26 a strong breeze sprung up, rapidly increasing
to a violent gale which lasted for three days and
played havoc with both personnel and material.
On the Peninsula and at Kephalo piers and break-
waters were broken up, causing an entire suspension
of communications; boats, lighters and barges
were sunk and wrecked. At the latter place a merchant ship, sunk to form a breakwater, had her
back broken and became a useless obstacle, her two
parts lying at an angle to each other. The gale was
accompanied by torrential rain that destroyed some
of our defensive works and trenches, drowning many
of their occupants, and to crown this disaster, a
blizzard ensued, freezing many men to death and
causing intense suffering to the troops in the trenches.
Some 10,000 casualties had, in consequence, to be
evacuated from the fighting line and there were more
than 200 deaths. Such a disaster would, at any
time, have been terrible, but coming, as it did, at
this critical and decisive moment, it was a catastrophe.

On November 28 I despatched my first telegram
of appreciation to the Admiralty. In it I explained
that the operation in view would be undertaken
for the purpose of opening the Straits and *keeping
them open*. To effect this, a squadron of eight battleships, four light cruisers and ten destroyers, with
four more older battleships, to act as supply vessels,

and merchantmen carrying coal and ammunition
—all fitted with mine bumpers—would enter the
Straits at dark, at such a time as to arrive above
the Narrows at earliest dawn. Under cover of
darkness and veiled from the searchlights on Kephaz
Point by a smoke screen, they would rush through
the mine-fields, past the Forts, and the first act of
the survivors would be the destruction of all depôts
on the beach and of the small craft capable of laying
mines, after which they would attack the forts, taking
them in reverse. A second squadron of six more
modern battleships, the *Lord Nelson*, the *Agamemnon*,
two King Edwards, the *Glory* and *Canopus* with
destroyers sweeping ahead of them, would attack the
Forts from below the mine-fields as soon as it was
sufficiently light ; whilst a third squadron, consisting of the *Swiftsure*, two monitors and five cruisers
would cover the Army and join in the attack on
the Forts from across the Peninsula. The co-operation of the Army was required to contain the Turkish
forces and prevent them from turning their mobile
artillery on to the ships and mine-sweepers ; and
herein lay the advantage we had gained from the
occupation of our present positions. I believe, I
added, that such a sudden attack, especially if, as
hoped, the enemy were taken by surprise, must
have a demoralizing effect on the Turkish Army
and on the population of Constantinople.

General Monro's answers to my questions were
not encouraging. The whole tone of his letter
betrayed a difference of mentality between us difficult of reconciliation. In it he set forth at length
that he considered little good could be hoped for
from the proposed action unless the ships could

exert direct pressure on the Turkish Army by naval
gunfire on its defensive positions or by throttling
the Turkish lines of supply of food and munitions.
He had little faith of considerable results accruing
from the former and did not believe that a squadron above the Narrows would make any far-reaching
impression on the main Turkish Army, for whatever
it might do in stopping supplies by day, it could
not do so by night. The effect produced would,
he thought, be mainly moral, and even that, in his
opinion, would not be great. He believed the Turks
would fight to the last to defend Constantinople
and that no mere menace would change their resolu-
tions. He would not count upon the destruction
of the defences of the Straits and always harped
upon the impossibility of keeping open the squadron
lines of communication. In answer to my second
question he considered that to gain the utmost
advantage, military action should be simultaneous,
but emphasized that the prospects of a general
offensive at the present time were not favourable.

After digesting the contents of this letter, I realized
that in him I had an opponent to our scheme who
would never deviate from his attitude of hostility
towards it, and were it to be sanctioned, it would
be against his advice.

On the military side of the question it was impossible for me to argue, but I could and did differ with
him on the feasibility of stopping enemy's supplies
and of securing the lines of communication of the
Fleet ; to my mind both would be the immediate
and almost automatic outcome of initial success.

That our power to stop the enemy's supplies was
no fallacy received practical proof only a few days

later. Ever since our submarine operations in the Marmora had so seriously hampered his sea communications these supplies had been reaching the Peninsula by means of a railway connecting the Turkish main system with Kavak, a small town at the head of the Gulf of Xeros; a bridge on this line was destroyed by gunfire by the *Agamemnon* on December 2, henceforth necessitating the remainder of the journey to be made by bullock wagons over a road impassable to motor traffic and exposed to fire from our submarines in the Marmora and from ships in the Gulf of Xeros.

A difference of opinion was also permissible as regards Turkish morale; there was no reason to suppose that it was higher than ours, for they had been content to remain inactive since the end of August and had made no attempt to eject us from our precarious positions, although considerably outnumbering us, unless indeed the cause of their inactivity was the hope of German assistance. In that case, however, all the more reason to bring off our coup before this assistance could arrive. I could not bring myself to believe that the presence of an Allied Fleet in the Marmora would be without moral effect; the threat, as we know, had been sufficient to cause a panic in Constantinople in March. Why should not the actuality do so now?

On November 30 I went to Kephalo for consultations with Generals Birdwood and Davies and Rear-Admiral Christian, who for some time past had been acting as Senior Naval Officer there. The scene that greeted the eye on entering the harbour was one of desolation, the result of the late gale. Its waters were still strewn with floating wreckage; of

the ship that had served as a breakwater only the
bows and stern were visible ; one part of the beach
had the appearance of a huge heap of scrap-iron,
for steamboats, lighters and barges were lying there
in inextricable confusion, heaped up one upon
another as though picked up from the water and
hurled by some giant hand indiscriminately on shore.

I informed the Generals of the proposed scheme.
General Davies was frankly opposed and could see
no good results likely to be gained. The attitude
of General Birdwood, owing to his fear of the political
results of evacuation, was less hostile. Naturally
enough he was hampered in his remarks by the knowledge of the Commander-in-Chief's opinions, but he
did say that a squadron of battleships above the
Narrows would improve the position at Suvla and
Anzac. General Byng was not present, but I knew
his views ; he had always believed evacuation
necessary and he was not likely to change his mind,
and I was left with no illusions as to the amount
of resistance I was likely to encounter. Nevertheless, so confident did I feel that success was obtainable and that opinions would undergo a complete
reversal, when the effects of naval power were once
realized, that I pursued my advocacy of our scheme
in spite of this strong military opposition.

Notwithstanding my hopes that evacuation would
not be resorted to, I did not lose sight of its contingency and concerted with General Birdwood as to
the steps that would in that case be necessary.

On December 2 I was made an acting Vice-Admiral.
This promotion strengthened my belief that de
Robeck would not return, a belief which seemed
further confirmed by an urgent telegram from the

Admiralty inquiring as to the time it would take to re-embark two divisions that had already been landed at Salonika and send them to Mudros—for it pointed to the Government lending a not unwilling ear to my proposals and contemplating a reinforcement of the troops at Gallipoli for the purpose of co-operation.

Encouraged by these signs I sent a personal telegram to the First Lord of the Admiralty (Mr. Balfour), developing my arguments in favour of a naval attack on the Straits, which, I pointed out, would under any circumstances stand an excellent chance of success ; but now this chance seemed enhanced by information received that the Turkish morale had been much shaken by the late blizzard and by the growing dislike with which German ascendancy was regarded at Constantinople ; and now, when all the world believed that we were about to evacuate the Peninsula, the chances of surprise and therefore of success were increased. I knew, I told him, that the General Commanding in Chief did not think the Army could attack with success, but I believed he under-estimated the effect of the presence of a naval force above the Narrows and controlling the Straits. Such being the case, I submitted that the naval attack be delivered with the understanding that the Army should be ready to take advantage of any favourable opportunity offered by its success and I ended by reiterating that the Turkish Army on the Peninsula would be cut off from Constantinople and when aware of this situation the effect upon them might be so great as to prove decisive even without the intervention of the Army.

On December 5 orders were received to suspend

all disembarkations at Salonika, and as a result of a
visit of Commander Keyes, whom I had sent there
to hasten matters, I was able to inform the Admiralty
that the time occupied to bring these troops to
Mudros would be considerably shortened.

All indications seemed to be pointing to the
fulfilment of our hopes, when on December 8 I
received a personal telegram from the Admiralty
announcing that : " In face of unanimous military
opinion H.M. Government have decided to shorten
front by evacuating Anzac and Suvla. . . ."

The blow was bitter and all the more so since
the heights to which our expectations had been
raised had been great. I had no illusions about
" shortening the front," whatever the ideas prevailing at Whitehall might be. I knew full well
that evacuation of Suvla and Anzac could only
herald that of Helles, must inevitably lead to retirement from the Peninsula and an inglorious termination of the campaign.

Convinced as I was of the soundness of my views,
I could not regard this fatal decision otherwise than
a disastrous mistake. Had it been the outcome of
the Admiralty's conviction that the forcing of the
Straits and keeping them open was an impracticable
proposition, I could have accepted it as the verdict
of a higher authority whose professional opinion
differed from mine and on whose shoulders the
responsibility ultimately rested. But was this the
case ? The manner in which my proposals had been
received and considered, the hesitancy with which
they had been finally rejected, seemed to show that
military opinion had prevailed and that the Western
school had gained the day. To what good the

sacrifice of invaluable lives and costly treasure squandered on the campaign if, at the last moment, victory was thus to be allowed to slip from our grasp ? That further naval action would have entailed heavy losses is probable, but the sacrifice would have been no greater than those offered up almost daily in the Western fronts with less chance of success; and can any one doubt that the results of a success here would have been more far-reaching than in any other theatre of the war ? Once through the Narrows an almost limitless vista opened out : Turkey would have been reduced to a negligible factor, Russia joined up with her allies, Egypt saved, our prestige in the East placed on an immutable basis and the end of the war brought within measurable distance at the cost of some ships incapable of facing the enemy's main fleet and of lives that their owners were only too ready and willing to give.

Such were the thoughts evoked in my mind by this momentous decision, and though I had no hopes of obtaining its reversal, I was determined that the Government should be fully acquainted with my views and therefore sent the following telegram to the First Lord :

" The reason given for this decision is a very great surprise to me, and one which I feel convinced has been arrived at under a misapprehension by the military at home : I have never seen any of the General Officer Commander-in-Chief's telegrams or appreciations, though I have shown him all of mine. I strongly confirm all I said in my telegram of November 28 *re* evacuation. The Navy is prepared to force the Straits and control them for an indefinite period, cutting off all Turkish supplies which now find their way to the Peninsula either by sea from the Marmora or across the Dardanelles from the Asiatic to the European shore. The only line of communications left would be the roads along the Isthmus of Bulair, which can be controlled almost entirely from the Sea of Marmora and the Gulf of Xeros.

" What is offered the Army therefore is the practical complete severance of all Turkish lines of communication accompanied by the destruction of the large supply depôts on the shores of the Dardanelles.

" In the first instance I strongly advocated that the naval attack should synchronize with an Army offensive ; but this is not a necessity, and if the Army will be prepared to attack in the event of a favourable opportunity presenting itself, nothing more need be required of them.

" The Navy here is prepared to undertake this operation with every assurance of success ! If the nets as described in your letter of November 24 can be provided these hopes of success are greatly increased and the possible losses greatly diminished.

" The unanimous military opinion referred to in Admiralty telegram No. 422 has, I feel certain, been greatly influenced, and naturally so, by the military appreciations of Sir Charles Monro. These I have not seen, but their purport I have gathered in course of conversations. The Corps Commanders, I know, view the evacuation with the greatest misgiving. The forcing of the Dardanelles, as outlined in my telegrams, has never been put before them and I am convinced that after considering the certain results which would follow a naval success, they would favour an attack on the lines indicated, especially in view of the undoubted low morale of the Turkish Peninsula Army of which we have ample evidence.

" A few days ago General Monro remarked to me : ' If you succeed and occupy Gallipoli, and even Constantinople, what then ? It would not help us in France or Flanders.' I mention this to show that he has quite failed to realize the significance of the real German offensive in the Near East. He is obsessed with the idea that the only method by which the Allies will be victorious is in killing or capturing such a number of Germans that they will be unable to continue fighting. He looks upon any action which does not have the above for its immediate objective as a waste of effort.

" The very extensive German propaganda being pursued all over the Near East accompanied by the expenditure of vast sums of money is not, I feel convinced, being undertaken merely as a side issue to the European War.

" A position of stale-mate on both fronts of the principal theatres of war appears the natural outcome of the present situation. This opinion is freely expressed in the higher military circles in Greece and would therefore appear to be fostered by the Germans—a significant point.

" By surrendering our position here, when within sight of victory, we are aiding the enemy to obtain markets the possession of which may enable her to outlast the Allies in the war of exhaustion now commencing.

" A successful attack would once and for all disperse these clouds of doubt, a large amount of

15

shipping would be released and the questions of Greece and Egypt settled.

" I do not know what has been decided about Constantinople, but if the Turk could be told that we were in the Marmora to prevent its occupation by the Germans, such a course would inevitably lead to disruption and therefore weakness amongst them.

" I fear the effect (of evacuation) on the Navy would be bad. Although no word of attack has passed my lips except to my immediate Staff and Admirals, I feel sure that every officer and man would feel that the campaign had been abandoned without sufficient use having been made of our greatest force, viz. the Navy.

" The position is so critical that there is no time for standing on ceremony, and I suggest that General Birdwood, the officer who would have to carry out the attack or evacuation which is now ordered, be asked for his appreciation.

" The logical conclusion therefore is the choice of evacuation or forcing the Straits. I consider the former disastrous, tactically and strategically, and the latter feasible, and, so long as troops remain at Anzac, decisive.

" I am convinced that the time is ripe for a vigorous offensive and I am confident of success."

This telegram brought forth two replies, a personal one from the First Lord and an official one from the Admiralty. The former ran as follows: " Your telegram has been very carefully considered. I personally agree with your appreciation of German designs in the East and I view with deepest regret the abandonment of Suvla and Anzac. But the military authorities, including Birdwood, are clear

that they cannot be made tenable against an increased
artillery fire, while the Admiralty hold that the
naval arguments against forcing the Straits are
overwhelming.   Naval authorities here are convinced
that, whilst success is most doubtful, very heavy
losses are certain, and it must be remembered that
nothing would have a worse effect on our Eastern
position than a serious check to the Navy.   This
would be represented as a heavy blow at our naval
supremacy.   In these circumstances, holding on to
Helles, taking only threatening (word missing)
and if possible attacking elsewhere seems best
course open to us."

In their official telegram the Admiralty informed
me they were not prepared to authorize the Navy
single-handed attempting to force the Narrows and
acting in the Sea of Marmora, cut off from supplies,
in view of individual and combined appreciation of
responsible Generals and the great strain thrown
on naval and military resources by the operations
in Greece, the Government's decision to evacuate
Suvla and Anzac would not be further questioned
by them.   This telegram ended with the following
sentence which caused me both surprise and anxiety :
" Holding Cape Helles and the mouth of the Straits
will enable another attack to be started later, working on a different plan, should the Government
decide to undertake it."

It was not apparently realized by the War Council
that the advantages accruing from the forcing
of the Straits depended upon the retention of our
positions on the Peninsula, whilst the possibility of
retaining these positions depended upon the forcing
of the Straits.   The two actions were interdependent,

abandonment of the one necessarily involved abandonment of the other. Sir Charles Monro had urged evacuation on account of the inability of his troops to attack with success and of the untenable position they would shortly be in owing to the advent of German reinforcements. When the Government therefore contemplated the retention of Helles, they could not have realized they were putting forward an impossible proposition, for by the evacuation of Suvla and Anzac the whole of the reinforced Turkish Army would be turned against Helles. Only by the capture of Achi-Baba or by the forcing of the Straits could our position there be secured, but the former so far had proved impracticable and the latter had now been vetoed.

These reasons induced me to address the following telegram to their Lordships on December 13 :

" On completion of evacuation of Suvla and Anzac a most serious situation will present itself at Helles.

" The whole of the Helles zone is exposed to artillery fire from the Asiatic shore and from the north of Achi-Baba. The intensity of this fire is likely to be more than doubled on account of the number of guns released from the northern zone and the influx of ammunition and heavy howitzers from Germany may cause it to become so severe as to force the Army to evacuate.

" The Helles position, even with the addition of heavy artillery, will be untenable unless the Army is in possession of Achi-Baba. The capture of this position appears to me essential if we are to retain our footing on the Peninsula.

" I consider the decision must be made at once and acted on without loss of time, and, if possible, before the Turks can move their artillery from Anzac and Suvla !

" A policy of holding on to our present position at Helles and waiting until Spring for offensive action will be suicidal for the Army. Better to evacuate that position immediately than to suffer a second and more decisive reverse by procrastinating.

" The capture of Achi-Baba position does not seem beyond our powers. The G.O.C. 8th Corps attributes the capture of trenches on November 15 with insignificant loss, to a great extent, to the support afforded by a Naval Squadron consisting of one specially protected cruiser and three monitors who, after careful registration used indirect fire without the assistance of spotting by aeroplanes, rendered impossible by high wind.

" Fifteen miles of heavy net is available here now ; with this it will be possible to guard an area off the left flank, where battleships will be able to lie and support the Army in a sustained attack.

" Once Achi-Baba is in our hands, we shall be in the position desired last April and the attack on the Narrows can be continued with every hope of success.

" I strongly hold that this is not a purely military matter, but one of combined naval and military importance, and I therefore have no hesitation in putting forward my views and consider it my duty to do so as the Admiral commanding at this critical moment."

According to my wont, I sent a copy of this telegram to Sir Charles Monro who, taking exception to my expressing an opinion on military matters, telegraphed to Lord Kitchener in that sense, a point of view with which I could not agree, and informed the Admiralty accordingly :

" General Monro has given me the copy of a telegram he has sent to Lord Kitchener with reference to my telegram of the 13th. He considers the question of the possibility of retention of our footing on Peninsula to be merely a military one. I regret I cannot concur in this. The important work of landing supplies for Army is a naval question, as is that of naval gun support. I am very surprised he does not consider that capture of Achi-Baba would reduce dangers which I anticipate from enemy's increased artillery fire. As an observation station alone it is invaluable to whoever holds it. It has always been talked of by higher military commanders as the key of the southern position. With it in our hands, Gully Beach would be available for landing stores, should increased fire from Asiatic batteries make this impossible on W and V Beaches. It would greatly increase effectiveness of naval gun-fire by giving us an ideal observation station where spotting from aeroplanes will be impossible owing to weather. The reported advent of heavy German artillery in northern zone has increased anxiety of military Commanders to evacuate as quickly as possible. It is hardly logical to neglect this contingency in the southern zone. Given suitable artillery, the enemy could drive supporting vessels out to a range from which their support would no longer be effective. The possession of Achi-Baba would permit ships to lie close in to Gully Beach and render effective support by firing over heads of our troops.

" General Monro states that the capture of Achi-

Baba is quite beyond our resources and he considers it a fruitless undertaking under existing military situation. I believe he under-estimates the support which, acting on the principles laid down by Sir Arthur Wilson, the whole Fleet can give in a general attack under present conditions and before enemy's artillery can be reinforced. If, however, his view is accepted, I am of opinion that evacuation of Helles should take place at once. To renew the attack after the enemy has had free access to arsenals of Germany for some time would, I fear, be attempting the almost impossible.

" General Monro has always shown me every consideration and we work together in greatest amity. I regret exceedingly that my views should differ from his, but I should be lacking in duty, were I not to place them fully before you."

In answer to this I received a personal telegram from the First Lord informing me that, though he agreed with my views, the possibility of the capture of Achi-Baba was a military and not a naval problem and that the Generals had unanimously arrived at the conclusion that it could not be taken by direct attack.

This was the last effort on my part to shape the course of events and there only remained to bow to the decision of the Government.

The whole of my attention was now turned towards that evacuation which I so dreaded, both on strategical and tactical grounds. The Head-quarter Staff had calculated the possible losses entailed in this operation at 30,000, and vaguely, with no data to work on, I had computed approximately the same, but should evacuation be interrupted by gales of

wind at any time during its last stages, there seemed
no limit to which the disaster might not attain. I
was haunted by the recollection of that heap of
derelict steamboats on the beach of Kephalo, and
I wished that I could bring that sight to the eyes
of those whose hesitancy and lack of vision had
brought us to this pass; for there was no shutting
one's eyes to the fact that however perfect the naval
and military arrangements might be, it would suffice
for one adverse factor—the weather—over which
we had no control, to produce a catastrophe.

This thought, though never uttered, was uppermost
in all our minds, and the two Staffs worked hard
and unremittingly at the preparations involving so
much elaborate detail, reminiscent of those days
ten months ago when we were occupied with other
plans somewhat similar but under such different
circumstances. Then, buoyed up by the hopes of
victory and with the minarets of Constantinople as
our goal, we were about to land an army; now, to
save the same force from destruction, we were about
to withdraw it; then, we could count on favourable
weather to assist us, now we could only expect
gales and hope that they might be averted. How
vain appeared now the sacrifices incurred! how
useless the loss of precious lives! Our earnest
prayer was that they should not be increased during
the final act of the tragedy.

General Birdwood's plans were based upon secrecy;
he hoped to be able to effect the evacuation of the
whole force without the enemy gaining any knowledge of his intentions and this necessitated holding
the trenches till the very last minute.

A gradual and systematic withdrawal of guns,

ammunition, stores, personnel and animals was commenced on December 10 and carried on nightly according to specific plans until the morning of the 18th, by which date all material capable of removal had been brought away and there remained some 40,000 men, equally divided between Suvla and Anzac, who had to be evacuated during the two following nights, together with such guns as were essential for holding the positions during these last critical hours. The small amount of stores incapable by that time of being removed were destroyed before the last of the troops came away.

To carry out these movements under the very eyes of an enemy in possession of the surrounding heights and provided with aeroplanes, without arousing his suspicions, required ingenuity and care. Every device therefore had to be resorted to to prevent his obtaining information. Nothing could be undertaken during the daylight hours indicating that anything unusual was afoot. Traffic between the Peninsula and the islands had to be neither more nor less than usual, the appearance of the beaches normal. To keep up the deception some mules were actually landed during these eight days, whilst gunfire was maintained at its ordinary volume in spite of the ever-decreasing number of guns.

On December 13, still flying my flag in the *Lord Nelson*, I proceeded to Kephalo, while Admiral Christian went to Mudros to superintend the many preparations necessary at the base. At Kephalo I remained in close consultation with General Birdwood until the evacuation was completed.

The nights of the 18th–19th and 19th–20th were fixed upon as those of the final stage. The trans-

portation of 43,000 men within the dark hours of
those two nights required the employment of an
amount of shipping that strained our resources to
the utmost. To avoid withdrawing ships from
Salonika, where their presence was urgently required,
I asked for and obtained the services of Admiral
Fremantle's squadron (H.M.S. *Zealandia*, H.M.S.
Hibernia and H.M.S. *Russell*). They arrived at
Mudros on the 14th and their ships' companies and
boats were a welcome addition to our means.

A flotilla of more than a hundred motor-lighters,
trawlers, steamboats and pulling boats were collected
at Kephalo by the 17th, from whence they would
be despatched to the different beaches for the conveyance of the troops to the vessels destined to carry
them away from the Peninsula. These consisted
of fourteen troop-carriers each holding, on an average, 1,200 men, two old battleships (the *Magnificent*
and *Mars*) sent from Egypt for the purpose, and two
light cruisers.

The large and unusual assemblage of small craft
at Kephalo would, had it come to the enemy's
knowledge, have warned him that some unusual
event was about to take place, and to prevent this
contingency, a strong and continuous aircraft patrol
was maintained in the Anzac and Suvla areas from
dawn to dusk, for the purpose of driving off any
hostile aeroplanes attempting to reconnoitre.

Captain Charles Corbett of the *Glory* and Captain
Hon. A. D. Boyle of the *Bacchante*, were in charge
of the naval arrangements at Suvla and Anzac
respectively, where, for several weeks, they had
been working in close co-operation with Generals
Byng and Godley and were thus intimately acquainted

with local conditions. The damage done at the beaches by the gale of November 27–28 entailed much extra labour ; piers had to be reconstructed and repaired and others added to allow the work of embarkation to be more expeditiously carried out. Moreover, the destruction on that occasion of the vessel forming the breakwater at Kephalo necessitated her replacement by another, for the protection of the innumerable small craft collecting in that harbour. A loaded collier was therefore carefully sunk and admirably fulfilled the requirements. Later on she was successfully raised without having sustained any damage either to herself or to her cargo.

As the last day of the occupation drew near the situation became more and more critical, and the anxiety of those on whom responsibility rested, proportionately greater. To General Birdwood's mind must ever have been present the possibility of an attack on his ever-diminishing forces whose powers of resistance hour by hour grew weaker. To me, the likelihood of a gale springing up and wrecking the last chance of our retreating troops was as a nightmare ; all the more ominous from the knowledge that such a catastrophe was not to be averted by any human agency. Had a southerly wind of even moderate force arisen at any time during the period of evacuation, piers must have wrecked, causing the embarkation to be carried out from open beaches and at heavy loss amongst the small craft, rendering anything in the nature of rapid evacuation an impossibility. Any attempt to cope with such an eventuality would have required a far larger reserve of small craft than was at our disposal. Interference by the enemy would have been calamitous owing to the beaches being fully exposed to shell-fire. Removal of the wounded would probably have been out of the question, and to meet this contingency arrangements were made to leave the hospital clearing stations intact with a proportion of the medical staff in attendance and thus ensure that our wounded would not suffer from want of attention. It was also arranged that under such circumstances an attempt was to have been made to negotiate an armistice on the morning after the evacuation to collect and, if possible, bring off our wounded.

The morning of the 18th broke fair and calm, giving promise of that fine weather so ardently desired. I began to feel some confidence in the successful issue of the precarious operation. At 9 p.m. I embarked in a destroyer and spent the night passing up and down the coast, watching and waiting for I hardly knew what ; but in truth there was little to see. All was still, not a sound was audible except an occasional burst of musketry such as might have been heard on any night during our occupation of the Peninsula. Twenty-one thousand men were being embarked, yet, except for the movement of the transports that glided noiselessly into their positions, eased down their anchors, took on board their quota of troops and as silently steamed off, to be succeeded in like manner by others, there was nothing to indicate to eye or ear that there was anything unusual going on. It had been so planned that never more than three transports were simultaneously in position off the beaches, and so accurately was the time-table adhered to, both by the troops and by the ships, that the arrangements were carried out to the minute and proceeded as smoothly as if they had been frequently practised. By 5.40 a.m. the night's work was over and at dawn all traces of this silent retirement had vanished.

The following day proved as fine as its predecessor and I felt that after a succession of ill-luck, fortune was at last favouring us. It was evident that the enemy had not the slightest idea of what was happening within earshot of him, and there was every reason to hope that the second night's proceedings might be as successful as the first.

The following twenty-four hours, however, were full of anxiety, especially for the Generals and troops in the now thinly manned trenches. So small a mischance might have betrayed the situation to the enemy and proved the cause of their annihilation.

In the evening I embarked in the light cruiser *Chatham* in company of General Birdwood and from the bridge of that ship lying off the Peninsula, awaited events. There was as little evidence of any great undertaking as there had been the night before, and the stillness was again only interrupted by the occasional sounds of firing. The transports arrived with the same silence and the same regularity; the whole operation was again carried out with the precision of a peace manœuvre. Little conversation passed between the General and myself, absorbed as we were in our thoughts. Mine reverted to that early morning eight months ago, when I stood on the bridge of another ship, beside another General, intently watching the gallant Lancashire Fusiliers as they had quietly got into the boats for the unfor-

getable attack on Helles. Now, as then, silence
and darkness were the prevailing features and it
was as difficult on this evening as it had been on
that morning, to realize that momentous events
were taking place. I thought of all the gallant
souls who had found their graves on the Peninsula
we were now abandoning and deplored the useless
sacrifice. I wondered how the Turks would employ
their army, released by this evacuation, and prayed
that our Government might yet awake to the true
state of affairs at Helles before it was too late. As
the hours crept slowly on and the embarkation
continued without any signs of incident, the load
of anxiety of the last few weeks seemed to fall away
and the certainty of a success, or at least of a disaster averted, gradually gained possession of me ;
the tension was past, moral fatigue gave way to
physical weariness, and I slept.

At 4.30 a.m. I was aroused by the receipt of a
pre-arranged signal from the beach at Anzac proclaiming the welcome news that the last man had
left the shore. At that moment there appeared
from the direction of Suvla the flare of fire—small
at first, but gaining in brilliancy until the sky was
reddened and the surroundings lit up. We steamed
towards the light and through my glasses I could
distinguish three large dumps of what must have
been abandoned stores burning furiously. Here
the troops had not yet all been embarked and I feared
that this conflagration might arouse the enemy to
a knowledge of what was going on and cause the
loss of the remnant still on shore. He showed no
signs of life, however, and when, at 5.40 a.m., the
last boat left the beach, dawn was just breaking,

showing up the hulls of the *Cornwallis* and *Glory* at anchor inside the net defence.

It was all over.   The evacuation was complete. Where a possible loss of 30,000 men had been computed, one only was missing ; and whether he was drowned or lost in the scrub, or accidentally killed was never ascertained.

This remarkable achievement was the result of a combination of circumstances ; faultless staffwork, perfect discipline, clever devices for hoodwinking the enemy, mutual confidence between officers and men, hearty co-operation between the two Services, and finally, good fortune as regards weather.   Had any one of these factors failed, the termination must have been far different.

How it was viewed by the enemy may be judged from the following translation of an article published in the *Vossische Zeitung* of January 21, 1916.

After describing the ground of the Peninsula as murderous the article proceeds :

" With the conquest of the beaches and the first line of the hills—for so far the English had got— they had gained nothing.   Under the infantry fire of the defenders holding the next ridge they would have to descend from the top of the hill into the valley, then storm the next hill and thus endlessly on.   The English had therefore probably realized the hopelessness of the struggle the last week of November, and about the middle of December had prepared their retreat in a manner so admirable as to call forth all praise.   As long as war exists their evacuation of the Arni Burnu and Anafarta fronts will stand in the eyes of all students of the strategy of retreat as a masterpiece which up to now has never been attained. A repetition of the *tour de force* did not, however, succeed on the South Front, according to the short Turkish report received up to now, as their embarkation there seems to have been accompanied by violent rear-guard engagements.

" I was privileged to witness the withdrawal from the West Coast under the most dramatic circumstances.

" The Commandant of the Austrian Howitzers (Mörser) Captain B. had proposed to the Commander-in-Chief of the Turkish Army operating in Gallipoli, Field-Marshal Liman von Sanders, to destroy an English Coast Battery which had made itself very unpleasantly felt, and had received orders to do so at 7 a.m. on December 20. The object was, if possible, to destroy it with the first shot so as to deprive the English artillerymen of the possibility of getting away, or still more, of getting their guns away. To obtain such a result it was only necessary to bring one of our howitzers into action, but it was important to find a suitable post of observation. To reconnoitre, Captain B. with the second in command of the battery, Upper Lieutenant H., started off at 3 p.m. on December 19 and I was allowed to accompany them. We motored until we arrived at the entrance of a narrow valley, in which stood a Turkish battery, and then ascended a long deep Turkish trench admirably constructed, until we reached the crest of the hill. The trench continued as far as the Turkish Infantry position and was as prettily laid out as the terrace of an hotel, the edge of it being neatly gravelled and planted with shrubs and brushwood. One could lean over and look down unhindered upon the English and the sea. And this sight was what perhaps most impressed me during the eighteen months of the war.

" There, on the shimmering sea, lay quiet and undisturbed the English men-of-war, torpedo boats and transports, as if no war existed. Nothing had interfered with them on their long passage out from England, nothing disturbed them here. Behind them rose, glittering out of the sea, the island of Imbros, one of the English bases. My eyes, unsuspicious as any of those on the Turkish side, received the impression of invincible might and greatness. Eighteen hours later I was indeed to realize how much of this had been a mirage. The battleships turned lazily and slowly round from time to time ; a flash, smoke, a reverberation. A broadside had been fired against the coast ; from time to time a torpedo boat fired too. Between ourselves and the sea rose low chains of hills on whose ridges English and Turkish infantry lay so close to one another that the enemies might almost have shaken hands. We were high enough not only to see the Ægean but over to the Hellespont on the other side, and through the translucent atmosphere it was easy to understand the genesis of so many legends and fables, of so many deeds and wonders, of Hero and Leander to the fantastic swim of Lord Byron—the wanderings of the Turks from Asia Minor—the irresistible longing of the Asiatics for the European Continent.

" Behind Suvla Bay, markedly outlined on the coast and separated from it only by a narrow strip of land, lies the Salt Lake, surrounded by the English Camp, i.e. by what we then believed to be the whole

16

English Camp. Twenty-four hours later, indeed, we knew better. White tents in beautiful rows, arranged in groups about earthworks thrown up for the Infantry and Artillery positions. Behind one of these earthworks, close on the beach, a flash of lightning appeared from time to time. Two hours had we been up there without moving a muscle. In fighting the English it is necessary to be very much on one's guard not to betray one's position, as they are past masters in the art of observation and in drawing conclusions from the veriest trifles. For two hours, therefore, we had taken care not even to put our noses over the parapet. But six eyes and three telescopes had anxiously scanned the track. And now there had been a flash, not much more than the glimmer of a match but the coast battery had betrayed itself. Captain B. hastily made a sketch of the position and stuck his visiting card on the wall of the trench to enable the telephone orderlies, who established the communication with the battery at night, to find the place easily. We then returned. As we were nearing the entrance of the valley, the hill behind us shook. The English had perhaps, after all, seen us. In any case they fired off a 30·5 cm. gun on to the hill, and a shell of quite respectable size fell close to us. Like children, we rejoiced at the prospect of the next day's shelling, but too soon.

" A bright moonlight night. Over and over again the warning of the outpost rang through our artillery camp—' Attention, Aviators ! '

" The night was very disturbed ; artillery fire as violent as I have only heard it so far in the battles on the Isonzo. We suspected an English attack.

" In the morning there was a thick white fog.
At 7 a.m. we wanted to start and ride up to our post
of observation, but Captain B. put off the firing
on account of the thick fog. Again we heard the
outposts call out ' Attention, Aviators ! ' and a few
bombs fell in the neighbourhood of the camp, without, however, doing any damage.

" Twice in the course of the next two hours did
we want to ride up and twice had we to dismount
on account of the fog.

" At 9 a.m. the officer in charge of the firing,
Upper Lieutenant F., called Captain B. to the
telephone, having just received a telephone message
from Headquarters. I heard the Captain shouting
down the telephone, ' What ! How ! Who ! ' then
he returned with a smile on his face : ' The English
have evacuated Gallipoli during the night ! ' Five
minutes later we were rushing as fast as the motor
would carry us to Headquarters. Turkish Staff
Officers turned out to meet Captain B. ; they shook
him warmly by the hand : ' You brought us luck,'
they said."

At Suvla nothing was abandoned to the enemy.
Four motor-lighters driven ashore on November
28 were destroyed by gunfire from the ships before
they steamed away. At Anzac a quantity of stores
which could not be taken away were piled up in
heaps on the beach, and as soon as it was light
enough, the *Chatham* opened fire with the object of
destroying them, while at the same moment the
enemy began a bombardment and the strange spectacle of the empty beach being heavily shelled by
friend and foe alike was to be witnessed.

The proximity of the enemy's positions and the

configuration of the ground rendered the task of the removal of stores far more difficult at Anzac than at Suvla, so that at the former ten guns, rendered unserviceable, and some sixty mules were left behind.

Aware of the intense anxiety with which the outcome of the evacuation was being awaited in England, I had arranged for a clear telegraph line and immediately despatched a message to the Admiralty announcing the results, and when I told the General of this, he laconically remarked that we had probably saved the Government ! Was that, I thought to myself, to be the only result of the campaign ?

I returned to Mudros on the 21st during a strong gale of wind which made me more grateful than ever for the escape we had had, to hear that de Robeck was expected on the following day and to receive a telegram offering me the command of the East Indian Station.

I left for England two days afterwards, but not before I had seen de Robeck, to whom I explained all that had happened ; the reasons that had led me to act as I did, and we parted the best of friends.

Helles was evacuated on January 8 under his supervision, but by that time my share of the Dardanelles campaign had come to an end.

CHAPTER XI

EIGHT years have now elapsed since the campaign of the Dardanelles was fought and lost, an interval of sufficient length to allow of an objective view of its inception, conduct and abandonment being taken by one who shared in all its hopes and illusions, in some of the excitement and much of the monotony.

Before understanding the true significance of this campaign, a comprehension of the political situation of Turkey and her relations to the belligerent Powers before the war is necessary, and this cannot be arrived at without some knowledge of the deep underlying causes that led to the European conflagration.

When from the war of 1870 Germany emerged a united Empire, she entered upon a period of unparalleled commercial and industrial prosperity, but in her transition from an agricultural into an industrial State soon found herself in need of colonies to provide her with raw materials and markets for the disposal of her manufactured goods. Of the former, however, there remained but few for her, the last come of the Great Powers, to occupy, and those she did acquire were invariably far distant and in many cases of a climate unsuited to a white race. Casting about in search of fresh fields for her colonizing activities Germany turned her eyes to the East and found, as she hoped, outlets for her

expansion in the policy generally known as that of
" Mittel-Europa," i.e., the linking up of Germany
and Austro-Hungary to Asia by means of the Balkans and Turkey. This was no new idea. Frederick
the Great had already sought a political entente
with the Ottoman Empire and in the forties of the
last century this policy had had two strong pro-
tagonists in von Moltke, then military attaché at
Constantinople, and Friedrich List, the well known
economist, who both urged its advantage, the former
on political and military—the latter on economic
grounds. Under the pressure of necessity therefore the colonization of Asia Minor and an access
to the markets of the East entered into the phase
of practical German politics. The Emperor Wil-
liam's famous journey to the Near East in the
autumn of 1898, his speech at the grave of Saladin
at Damascus, were but the foreshadowing of the
realization of that great dream, a German Austrian
Turkish Empire extending from the mouth of the
Elbe to that of the Euphrates, while the first practical step towards its fulfilment was the construction
of the Bagdad Railway, the concession for which
was to be signed a year later.

Here then was a clear German policy aiming at
the creation of a great economic unit whose influence would extend from Hamburg to Basra with
tentacles reaching to the Baltic, the North Sea, the
Adriatic and the Ægean.

Though desirous of the economic exploitation of
Turkey, it was Germany's interest to uphold that
country's political integrity and here her policy ran
directly counter to that of Russia, who ever since
the days of Peter the Great had regarded the posses-

sion of Constantinople and the Dardanelles as the goal of her desires, not only on religious and nationalist grounds but as being the Gate of the Black Sea on whose shores are situated her only warm water ports. But besides being a menace to Russian ambition this policy—Berlin Bagdad as it came to be called—was a direct thrust at our Indian Empire ; a threat on the flanks of our communications with the East. Hence German aims came into direct opposition to the interests both of England and Russia, and however later events may have temporarily obscured the true issues of the European struggle these cardinal facts should never be lost sight of, for though this contest was eventually to be fought out on French soil it was on the shores of the Bosphorus that the key of the whole situation was to be found.

In the meanwhile, ever pressed by her needs for expansion, Germany was endeavouring to gain a foothold in Morocco, endeavours which were rendered abortive by the prior claims of France and which nearly led to war ; whilst after the incident of Agadir her attempts to come to an amicable arrangement with the latter Power over the Congo were also doomed to failure. On the other hand the efforts of Russia, backed by those of the Western Powers, to create a Balkan Federation as a barrier to the German advance to Constantinople were wrecked by Serbo-Bulgarian rivalry.

These moves and counter moves on the part of the Great Powers created a political situation surrounded by an atmosphere of suspicion and fear that rapidly got beyond human control and could only be solved by an appeal to arms.

That Turkey would not remain supine during a conflict in which her very existence was at stake was beyond a doubt, and the reproach of treachery so often levelled at her, is hardly justified by facts. Turkey fought as she always had fought against Russia, and if in 1914 she was ranged by the side of Germany against her ancient allies England and France, it was because they now were the allies of her hereditary foe.

France, of all the Powers the one least interested in these conflicting issues, was drawn into the vortex by her alliance with Russia, and it is the irony of fate that she, the least concerned, should have been the greatest sufferer. When, then, in the autumn of 1912, the Balkan war broke out, those responsible for the conduct of affairs throughout Europe can have had no illusions as to the danger that was threatening the peace of the world, nor any doubts but that a war of unparalleled magnitude was merely a question of time.

On looking back at these critical years before the war one cannot now but be amazed at the diplomatic neglect into which Constantinople, the very storm centre, had been allowed to fall by our Government, and at the lack of foresight with which the situation was handled. For more than eighteen months peace had been hanging by a thread and yet, when six weeks after the assassination of the Archduke Franz Ferdinand—an event universally regarded as the signal for the outbreak of hostilities—war was declared, the British Ambassador at Constantinople was absent from his post and the Embassy apparently as unaware of the negotiations going on during the July crisis between Germany and the Young

Turk party, as of the alliance between the two
States signed on August 2.

To this ignorance must be attributed the escape
of the *Goeben* and *Breslau* with all its fateful consequences. The responsibility for this unhappy incident has often been discussed and variously attributed ; but of the diplomatist who failed to keep
his Government informed of such weighty happenings, of the Admiralty who issued confusing and
contradictory orders—or of the Admiral who omitted
to take precautions against an unsuspected danger
of whose existence he could not possibly be aware,
who was to blame ?

This failure in the sphere of diplomacy had its
counterpart, perhaps naturally, in a lack of anticipation of military action in the Near East. The
escape of the *Goeben*, and Turkey's entry into the
war may have opened the eyes of the Government
to the probability that action against that power
would sooner or later have to be resorted to, but
neither of these events appear to have caused them
to make any preparations for such an eventuality.

One would have expected to learn that the Dardanelles Campaign had been put into execution as
a preconceived plan, part of the higher strategy of
the war ; that it had been undertaken with the
object of frustrating Germany's well-known aims,
of defeating an isolated enemy and, by opening
communications with Russia, of assuring the export
of her wheat and permitting of her being supplied
with the munitions of which she was so sorely in
need. But as we shall see, such was not the case.
The attack on the Dardanelles was undertaken at
the invitation of Russia as a " demonstration " to

divert from the Caucasus Turkish troops that were pressing her hardly there.

The campaign has been severely criticized as an operation of war undertaken in violation of the fundamental principles of strategy which teach that concentration of all available force on the main field of battle is the surest means of attaining victory. Initiated and conducted as it was the criticism is perfectly justified, for, in the eyes of the War Council, it never attained to the footing of a major operation but was always conducted by them as a minor one, subsidiary to the campaign in France. As such it diverted from that theatre of the war, which they always regarded as the main one, troops and munitions in quantities large enough to greatly hamper the plans of the Allied Generals on the Western front, but insufficient to assure success in Turkey; whilst there is, I believe, a consensus of military opinion that had Sir Ian Hamilton from the commencement been supplied with shell in a proportion equal to that of Sir John French the results would have been very different to what they actually were.

But before any just appreciation of the circumstances attending its conception can be arrived at a survey of the general situation at the time must be taken.

The war had then been raging for more than six months. The fallacy that no nation was capable of supporting a prolonged struggle had already been exploded, and it was just beginning to dawn upon shocked mankind that the entire strength and resources of the belligerent nations would have to be developed and brought into use before victory could be looked for. Neither Italy, nor the United States, Bulgaria, Roumania nor Greece had yet entered the arena, and to gain the alliance of all or any one of these neutrals—or failing their alliance, to prevent them from joining the enemy—was a matter of such vital importance both to the Allies and to the Central Powers as to profoundly influence the actions of either when dealing with matters affecting these countries.

At sea the submarine campaign had not yet assumed the serious proportions that it afterwards attained; the German High Sea Fleet was contained in the Heligoland Bight by the Grand Fleet; the Austrian Squadron in the Adriatic was similarly held by the French Naval Forces in the Mediterranean, whilst the destruction of Von Spee's Squadron off the Falkland Isles had cleared the ocean of enemy cruisers and given to the Entente Powers that command of the sea that made possible the despatch of troops to any destination. In France, the scene of the main struggle, the German advance had been brought to a standstill, and the enemies stood face to face deeply entrenched in a line reaching from the English Channel right across the Continent to the frontiers of Switzerland—a line impossible of being outflanked and seemingly incapable of being pierced by either side without such a preponderance of force as neither could bring on the scene for a long time to come.

Under these circumstances it was but natural that those responsible for carrying on the war should search for other theatres where a more rapid decision might be hoped to be reached; but the Entente Powers were suffering from the difficulties inherent

to all alliances—a lack of a central authority for
the conduct of the war. It is true that they all had
a common end in view—the defeat of the enemy
—but when the means of attaining this end came
to be discussed differences of opinion, difficult of
reconciliation, inevitably arose. That French and
Belgian territories were in the occupation of the
enemy and that the population of these territories
were suffering from the organized brutalities of the
German armies was a reason sufficient for causing
our Allies to regard the matter from a less objective
point of view than could we, whose shores had not
been subjected to invasion, and there consequently
arose two schools of thought—one regarding any
action tending to divert troops from the French
front as a misapplication of force and a waste of
energy—the other holding the opinion that the only
chance of victory lay in holding the enemy on the
Western Front and concentrating all forces not
required for this purpose for an attack in some other
theatre. Those belonging to the latter school
believed that they saw in a thrust at Constantinople
through an onslaught on the Dardanelles a means
of attaining their end. Unfortunately the War
Council—a body composed of a selected number of
Cabinet Ministers consisting of the Prime Minister
(Mr. Asquith), The Lord Chancellor (Lord Haldane),
The Secretary of State for War (Lord Kitchener), the
First Lord of the Admiralty (Mr. Winston Churchill),
the Secretary of State for Foreign Affairs (Sir Edward
Grey), the Secretary of State for India (Lord Crewe),
the Chancellor of the Exchequer (Mr. Lloyd George)
—to whom the conduct of the war had been entrusted,
proved itself unequal to the task of coming to any

definite decisions between these conflicting ideas, and it will be seen how by adopting a compromise they allowed themselves to drift into a campaign costly, bloody and ineffective which, had it been duly studied, properly prepared and only commenced when the necessary troops were available, held promise of brilliant results.

If we follow the course of events which ultimately led to the landing of those glorious troops on the Gallipoli Peninsula on April 25, 1915, we shall see how unsuitable is a large body of men, however capable they may individually be, for the supreme task of waging war ; and we shall moreover learn with some astonishment that professional opinion had but little effect upon their decisions.

Turkey declared War on October 31, 1914, and three days later an Anglo-French Squadron that had been watching the Dardanelles ever since the escape of the *Goeben* to Constantinople, bombarded the forts at the entrance of the Straits. No part of any preconcerted plan, this was merely a spasmodic act on the part of the Admiralty, undertaken for the purpose of drawing the enemy's fire and ascertaining the range and power of his guns. It is in itself evidence that at that time there existed no plans for any attack such as was later to be delivered. But the idea of some such operation must have been in the minds of some of the War Council, even if only as the result of this isolated action, and it is strange therefore that steps should not have been taken to have the matter studied, by both the Naval and Military Staffs ; all the more so since on November 25 the possibility of forcing the Straits was, if somewhat perfunctorily, discussed. The matter

then, however, was deemed unfeasible on account
of the lack of available troops. It is interesting
to note that on this occasion Mr. Winston Churchill
expressed the view that any attempt on Constantinople was an undertaking of great difficulty and
required a large military force to carry it out, a
principle which hardly coincides with his action·a
few months later ; whilst Lord Kitchener did not
view it unfavourably owing to its being a possible
means of arresting an invasion of Egypt.

On January 2, 1915, the subject was once more
brought to the fore owing to an appeal from Russia,
whose armies in the Caucasus were then being
hardly pressed by the Turks. She asked that some
diversion should be made which would have the
effect of drawing off the Turkish troops to another
scene. That our Government should be anxious to
comply with a request from an Ally who had successfully performed a similar service in the early
part of the war at great sacrifice to herself, was but
natural ; and a reply was sent promising we would
do what we could. But how could such a promise
be carried out ? There were no troops available
for the purpose, and though a squadron of battleships could be assembled for attacking the forts of
the Dardanelles, a purely naval effort was not
likely to have the desired effect, for even had an
attempt to force the Straits proved as successful as
its most enthusiastic supporters desired, the Fleet
alone, without an army to occupy Constantinople,
could do but little, even when it had forced its way
into the Marmora. It would have been able to
destroy the Turkish Fleet, it would even have been
in a position to destroy the city, and its presence

would certainly produce a panic amongst the inhabitants; the Government might capitulate or fly to Asia Minor, but without troops there would be only ruin and massacre and a mere naval success would be void of any tangible results—and no troops were available.

In view of the impossibility of fulfilling the promise in any other way, Lord Kitchener suggested that a "demonstration" should be made against the Dardanelles, and Mr. Churchill seized upon the proposal to develop the idea, not only of attacking the forts, but of attempting to force a passage through the Straits; and who shall blame him for this conception which, if properly carried out, would have led to such brilliant results? If only he could have been brought to realize that simultaneous military co-operation was essential, if only he could have been brought to direct all his talents and great energies towards securing a combined operation, having for its object the forcing of the Straits by the capture of the Gallipoli Peninsula, a different story might have had to be told; for it cannot be too clearly realized that even had his belief in the possibility of the Fleet passing into the Marmora proved correct, the Peninsula of Gallipoli would have had to be in our hands before its lines of communication could have been made secure; and if Constantinople was to have been occupied, and not merely destroyed by the guns of the Fleet, an army also must have accompanied the Squadron into the Sea of Marmora.

On the following day, January 3, a telegram was sent from the Foreign Office to our Ambassador in St. Petersburg, authorizing him to inform the

Russian Government that a demonstration would
be carried out, but at the same time stating that
it could hardly be expected to cause a withdrawal
of Turkish troops from the Caucasus.

Thus were we pledged to action against Turkey
without any clear conception of eventualities
entailed, without reference to the Staffs whose combined study of the subject could not have failed to
bring to light the difficulties of the problem.

The first step in the direction of that quicksand
in which we were so nearly to be engulfed had
unwittingly been taken.

Mr. Churchill lost no time in communicating with
Admiral Carden, then commanding the Squadron
at the mouth of the Dardanelles, who, in reply to
questions put to him gave his opinion that although
the Straits could not be " rushed," the forts might
be destroyed by an extended operation. The first
Lord informed him that " High Authorities here "
concurred in his opinion, but who those High Authorities were is not clear and no gunnery experts
appear to have been consulted. Admiral Carden's
plans contained proposals for the destruction of the
forts at the entrance to the Straits, for the destruction of the defences of the Narrows and for sweeping
a channel through the mine fields, and the time
estimated for carrying them out was one month.
Admiral Sir Henry Jackson, at that time working
on the Staff of the Admiralty, but in no position of
authority or responsibility, in a memorandum that he
wrote at the First Lord's instance laid stress on the
fact that in the event of the Fleet getting through
to the Sea of Marmora it would be cut off from its
supplies unless the Gallipoli Peninsula was in our

hands, and that although Constantinople would be at the mercy of our guns, the city could not be occupied without a large military force. He (Sir Henry) only concurred in the attack on the outer forts.

In spite of this clear note of warning, Admiral Carden's proposals—limited though they were to the purely naval and tactical side of the larger strategical problem—appealed strongly to Mr. Churchill, to whose sanguine temperament they held out a hope of advancing his desires; and at a further meeting of the War Council on January 13, he reported all that had passed between the Admiralty and Admiral Carden and showed that ships suitable to the enterprise were available, including the new *Queen Elizabeth*—then at Gibraltar carrying out her gun trials. This ship, the first to carry 15-inch guns, played no inconsiderable part in the development of events, for a somewhat exaggerated idea of her powers enabled Mr. Churchill to overcome Lord Kitchener's reluctance to the undertaking of a purely naval attack.

At this memorable meeting neither Lord Fisher, Sir Arthur Wilson nor Sir James Wolf-Murray (C.I.G.S.) were called upon for their opinions, nor did they make any remarks, and the silence of the two former permitted of Mr. Churchill's taking their acquiescence for granted. After hearing the views of Lord Kitchener and of Mr. Churchill the War Council arrived at a decision that was embodied in the following astounding memorandum: " The Admiralty should prepare for a naval expedition in February to bombard and take Gallipoli Peninsula with Constantinople as its objective."

17

The procedure at this meeting was not such as to beget confidence in the ability of the Council to carry out the duties entrusted to it. From evidence given before the Dardanelles Commission it transpired that a considerable difference of opinion existed amongst those who were present as to whether any direct decision had been arrived at or not! Mr. Asquith, the Prime Minister, understood that the Council was pledged to nothing more than preparations; Mr. Churchill on the other hand regarded the decision as the approval of a principle, whilst Lord Crewe believed that the operation was "approved subject to the occurrence of any unforeseen event which might have made it from one point of view unnecessary." Sir James Murray left the Council with very indistinct impressions on the matter, but Lord Fisher believed that approval of the operation had been given.

Thus was a question involving the most tremendous issues handled in such a manner as to leave it in utter confusion, a confusion characteristically reflected by the wording of the memorandum. How could the Admiralty prepare to take Gallipoli Peninsula? That was a military—or more accurately a combined naval and military operation, but since no troops were forthcoming the order was perfectly meaningless. And what was meant by the phrase, "With Constantinople as its objective?" Apparently the capture of the famous city was in the minds of the authors of this document, but how this feat was to be accomplished without troops is not clear.

That the First Sea Lord on whom, according to the constitution of the Admiralty, the responsibility for operations lay, should acquiesce in an operation in whose success he had no faith, is a fact only to be accounted for by the ascendancy of political over naval and military influence, an instance of professional knowledge allowing itself to be overridden by political expediency.

As to the memorandum itself, it is difficult to imagine any way of expressing an order, a thought, a desire—call it what you may—more likely to lead to misconception or confusion, and as we have just seen, that was exactly the effect produced on those concerned, and it must for ever remain a monument of the ineptitude of the Council in whose hands lay the conduct of the War.

At a further meeting of the Council on January 28, it became apparent that Mr. Churchill's optimistic anticipation of the results of the proposed attack had done much to colour the views of his colleagues. Mr. Balfour said that it was difficult to imagine a more hopeful operation ; Sir Edward Grey hoped that it would settle the attitude of Bulgaria and the Balkans; and Lord Kitchener believed that success would be equivalent to a successful campaign of the new Armies. Lord Fisher, the only man present whose professional knowledge enabled him to form a sound judgment of the probable result, maintained a hostile silence, whilst the effects of victory were being discounted. Previously to the meeting he and the First Lord had had an interview with the Prime Minister at which he had laid forth his views on the naval policy, and he attended the Council in the belief that a final decision on the matter was not to be taken that day. When, therefore, he realized that

such was not to be the case he got up from the table
with the intention of leaving the meeting and of
tendering his resignation. But Lord Kitchener
waylaid him and in a conversation held apart, after
pointing out that he was the only man present who
disagreed with the proposal, eventually persuaded
him to resume his seat. The meeting adjourned
until late in the afternoon, and during this interval
Mr. Churchill urged Lord Fisher to acquiesce in the
proposal and he consented, so that when the Council
reassembled in the afternoon Mr. Churchill was
able to announce that, with Lord Fisher's agreement,
the Admiralty had decided to undertake the operation.

And so the die was cast. The second step in
that succession of events which formed the tragedy
of the Gallipoli Campaign had been taken ; with
the assent, it is true, but the reluctant consent, of
the First Sea Lord and against his better judgment.

When we reflect upon Lord Fisher's triumphant
naval career, the high-handed manner in which he
had ever borne down all opposition, and how he
had succeeded in imposing his reforms upon a conservative service in face of established tradition and
deep prejudice, we cannot but wonder that on such
a momentous question he should have allowed his
better judgment to be over-ruled. That he was not
a member of the War Council, and therefore technically not responsible for any of its decisions, does
not seem to offer a sufficient explanation of a man
of his character acquiescing in the proposal which
his professional knowledge told him was unlikely
to be crowned with success. We know that he,
like the politicians, believed that the operations

could be broken off at any convenient or suitable moment, but considering that one of the reasons of its being undertaken was the belief that its success would tip the Balkan balance in our favour, it was obvious that its failure would have the opposite effect. Its voluntary abandonment, therefore, without a far greater expenditure of effort than he or indeed any member of the War Council were at that time disposed to expend upon it, was highly improbable.

The decision once taken matters developed in a manner unexpected by the War Council ; it was gradually realized that in spite of the ruling that the attack was to be delivered by the Navy alone, the presence of some military force, however small, would be necessary if only for the purpose of demolishing the forts after they had been silenced by the guns of the Fleet. Lord Kitchener, who always asserted that no troops would be available for the enterprise, relaxed his attitude to the extent of declaring on February 9 that " if the Navy required the assistance of land forces at a later stage that assistance would be forthcoming." Such a declaration from such a quarter could only be regarded as admitting the possibility of the Navy being unable to accomplish the task allotted to it. It also showed that the theory of its abandonment when desired was untenable. Beyond pushing forward the naval preparations nothing further was done until February 16, when at a meeting of Ministers—not, it would seem, a meeting of the properly constituted War Council—it was decided that the 29th Division, hitherto destined for the French front, should be sent to Lemnos as soon as possible and that a portion of the troops then in Egypt should be held in readiness to be despatched to the same destination if required. These forces were to be regarded as available to support the naval attack on the Dardanelles in case of necessity and, furthermore, the Admiralty were empowered to build special transports and lighters suitable for landing a force of 50,000 men at any required point. If even now, when a definite number of troops were actually earmarked for use at the Dardanelles, the situation had been reconsidered with a view to a combined operation the chances of success would have been greatly increased, for the Turk was still but ill-prepared for an invasion of the Gallipoli Peninsula. But a niggardliness of spirit which hesitated to throw all available force into the attack, prevailed, and the Navy was allowed to commence the operation which professional opinion considered problematical of success, without that military assistance which was actually available. Never was war waged in a more half-hearted manner.

A point had now been reached when an operation was about to be commenced which had for its object the forcing of the Straits. On the spot were naval forces deemed sufficient for the purpose : under orders to proceed to the scene of action some 80,000 troops, but these were only to be used in case of necessity. No serious study had been made as to the manner in which they could be employed either in conjunction with the Fleet or, in case of its success, after it had forced its way into the Sea of Marmora. No estimate had been made of the amount of opposition likely to be encountered in either case. The War Council seems to have been quite unaware that they were slowly but surely allowing themselves to drift into a situation from which they would be unable to extricate themselves without loss of prestige or that expenditure of life and treasure that they were so anxious to avoid. They were seemingly content to trust to good fortune to make up for their want of resolution—which itself heralded failure—and to hope that luck would compensate for lack of foresight. But success is not to be won by such methods as these, and when eventually, on March 18, it was proved that the forcing of the Straits could not be accomplished by naval forces alone, the Admirals and Generals on the spot found themselves without any preconceived plans and in ignorance of the intentions of the Government at home.

In the meantime, whilst the troops were on their way, the first phase of Admiral Carden's plan was put into execution. The bombardment of the outer forts was commenced on February 19, but owing to bad weather was only completed on the 25th, by which time, with the aid of demolition parties supplied by a Marine Brigade sent from England for the purpose, they were completely destroyed, enabling the Admiral to continue the prosecution of the second phase of his operations.

General Birdwood, commanding the Australian and New Zealand troops in Egypt under orders for the Dardanelles, was instructed to proceed to Lemnos in order to confer with the Admiral and to form an appreciation of the situation. But any idea of combined operations was still deprecated, for the General was told that his troops should only be employed in such minor operations as the final destruction of batteries after they had been silenced by the guns of the Fleet, or dealing with concealed guns incapable of being located by the ships, if called upon to do so by the Admiral. The General arrived on March 1 and as a result of his conferences with the Admiral and of his own observations, reported that he did not believe in the ability of the Fleet to force the passage unaided and that he anticipated that major military operations would be necessary to deal with the formidable character of the defences of the Peninsula. The warning fell on deaf ears. The naval attack was allowed to proceed without any modification of plan on the part of the Authorities in England, and the General returned to Egypt to put in hand preparations of plans—the greater part of which should have already been accomplished in England.

The original blunder of commencing the bombardment before military assistance—" in case of necessity "—was at hand now became apparent. As the second phase of Admiral Carden's plans developed it became increasingly evident that the difficulties had been under-estimated. The concealed batteries on the Peninsula were proving a more formidable obstacle to mine-sweeping than had been anticipated, and could only be dealt with by military forces. But these were not ready, even had it been permissible to use them. Had the troops which began to arrive at Lemnos in the early days of March been despatched in a state of preparation for action : had the transports not been obliged to go to Alexandria for reorganization : had previously prepared plans been forthcoming—the military attack might have been delivered at this critical moment and the whole course of events taken a different and favourable turn.

Sir Ian Hamilton, who had been appointed Commander-in-Chief of the troops early in March, arrived in time to witness what proved the Fleet's last effort on the 18th. His instructions were framed in the same spirit of compromise as characterized the whole conception of the campaign. He had been told that the Fleet had undertaken to force the passage of the Straits and that the employment of military forces on any large scale was only to be contemplated in the event of it failing in its task after every effort had been exhausted. It was impressed upon him that once the project had been entered upon no idea could be entertained of abandoning the scheme, and that it was essential to avoid a check which would jeopardize the chances of strategical and political success, and that any such minor operations as clearing areas occupied by Turkish guns annoying the Fleet or demolition of already silenced forts should not, if possible, entail permanent occupation of positions on Gallipoli Peninsula. No information had been furnished by the War Office Staff, no preliminary plan or scheme of operations had been drawn up. As he himself said in his evidence before the Dardanelles Commission: "The Army Council had disappeared." But in a conversation held with Lord Kitchener before leaving England the latter had explained that he hoped the Fleet would get through without Sir Ian's help and that he contemplated landing the troops on the shores of the Bosphorus.

But there was work for them to do before the Bosphorus could be reached. After every effort had been exhausted the naval attack broke down, and if the operation were not to be abandoned (and Sir Ian's instructions show that on this matter, at any rate, the Government had at length changed its mind) the moment had arrived, so disconcerting to the War Council's plans but not unexpected by the Naval Staff, when military assistance must be called in.

Any immediate attempt, however, to throw the Army on shore was out of the question. The enemy was thoroughly on the alert and any chance that might previously have existed of taking him by surprise had now vanished. The Commander-in-Chief had had no opportunity of studying the situation or of formulating any plans, and the success of such an undertaking depended upon most detailed and elaborate organization. All further operations therefore had to be postponed until such time as these were drawn up, and Sir Ian proceeded to Egypt, followed by those transports that had not already gone there.

All chance of secrecy had disappeared and it could only be hoped that the withdrawal of the troops from Lemnos might lead the enemy to believe that the failure of March 18 had caused the attack to be abandoned.

CHAPTER XII

WAR is but the forcible means of attaining those ends which diplomacy has failed to secure and can only be brought to a successful issue if naval, military and political action have a common direction.

In the days of a Frederick the Great or of a Napoleon this singleness of purpose was achieved by the concentration of military executive and political direction in one person, but in an age of democracy, when this is manifestly impossible it can only be attained by close co-operation between the naval, military and political elements and by a nice balance of their respective responsibilities. But though the system of conducting war by councils or committees is the only one possible under democracy, it has many disadvantages and is rarely fraught with good results. In any such body differences of opinion are bound to arise only capable of being adjusted by compromise; and compromise, advantageous and even necessary as it is in political life, is disastrous in war. The evil is augmented when, as was the case in 1914, the Council (with the exception of Lord Kitchener) consists of political elements only. Neither the First Sea Lord nor the Chief of the Imperial General Staff were members; they attended the meeting as professional advisers only. But advice without responsibility loses most of its value, and if the naval and military points of view of naval and military operations are only to be put forward by officers whose responsibility ends with an exposition of their opinions, their views cannot carry the weight that is their due when technical matters—i.e., naval and military operations, are under discussion. The fact that the Secretary of State for War was an eminent soldier, whilst the First Lord of the Admiralty was a civilian, and that the First Sea Lord—a sailor —was nothing more than a technical adviser and not a member of the War Council, was in itself sufficient to disturb that balance of responsibility on which rested the whole efficiency of the Council, and never was this more clearly evidenced than during the discussions on the attack on the Dardanelles. A naval operation, it was proposed by a soldier as the only means at hand of easing a distant military situation; as such it was enthusiastically taken up by a civilian as likely in his opinion of attaining a political end—the occupation of Constantinople—while the only hesitating voice was that of the naval expert who saw no prospect of its fulfilling either object without military assistance.

These facts throw into high relief the dangers arising from the composition of the War Council, for, although all were agreed as to the advantages that the success of the operation would procure, the only man whose professional knowledge enabled him to form a sound judgment as to the chances of that success was handicapped by having no voice in the decision. We have seen how Lord Fisher, just because he was *not* a member of the War Council, refrained from speaking his mind at its meetings on January 23 and 28, and it is justifiable to infer that had he been invested with the authority and responsibility of a member, his objections would not have been so easily over-ruled. As it was, the War Council appear to have taken it for granted that Mr. Churchill's advocacy of the project implied Admiralty approval, but had they made closer inquiries they would have found that, although Lord Fisher was eventually brought to give his acquiescence, it was with misgivings ; and that the Staffs, naval and military, had made no recent joint study of the subject, though some years previously the operation had been pronounced unfeasible by the Council of Imperial Defence. Thus we see how by erroneous composition of the body in whose hands lay the conduct of the war, difficulties that might have been obviated developed into real dangers. This probably would not have happened had Lord Fisher and Sir James Wolfe Murray been, or considered themselves to have been, in a position to put forward their views clearly and at length ; for even had the War Council over-ridden their objections, its members would at least then have been under no illusions as to the nature of the difficulties that confronted them and might have been saved from drifting into the inextricable position in which they afterwards found themselves. At the same time it must ever remain a matter of surprise that a man of Lord Fisher's autocratic temperament and outstanding position should not have, in spite of the ambiguous situation he was placed in, made greater efforts to give expression to the feelings of disapproval with which he regarded the proposal.

Had, however, the Council possessed all those qualities for the direction of the war which as we have seen they so conspicuously lacked, they would still have been confronted with a source of danger in the organization of the Admiralty that was gradually proving itself unsuitable for the conduct of the naval war ; a danger all the greater as at the outset it was unsuspected.

The Board of Admiralty, as it existed in 1914, was a creation of 1832, and although it had proved itself an efficient body for the administration of the naval service during those eighty-two years, it had never undergone the test of a great naval war. During that period it had successfully exercised towards the Navy many of the functions that in the military service were the province of the War Office and the Horse Guards and the Commander-in-Chief in the field. It was charged with two distinct duties, equally important but materially different : the direction of Naval Forces and their production and maintenance. Prior to 1832 these two separate functions had been performed by two separate bodies, the Admiralty Board and the Navy Board, and it was under this dual system that all our great naval wars had been fought.

After the Napoleonic wars there arose the same need for economy as there did after the Armistice of 1918, which eventually led Sir James Graham, at that time First Lord of the Admiralty, to merge the two bodies into one: the Board of Admiralty as at present constituted. Each of the members of this new Board was directly responsible for some part of the duties previously performed by the two old Boards. Under the older system there had been a distinct cleavage between the two, symbolized by their being located under two separate roofs ; conduct of war was the duty of the Admiralty Board, production of supplies and material that of the Navy Board. In the language of to-day the old Admiralty Board was the Staff, the old Navy Board a Maintenance Committee. But under Sir James Graham's new organization this division disappeared, giving way to a concentration of executive and administrative powers in the reconstructed Single Board of Admiralty.

After a very short experience of hostilities, it grew increasingly apparent that this organization, effective though it had proved itself in peace, did not fulfil the requirements for war. It was found impossible for the Sea Lords to carry out the duties of a general direction of operations, formerly the province of the Admiralty Board, and at the same time their duties of production and maintenance, the functions of the old Navy Board. As the result of this incapacity there was evolved a "War Staff Group" consisting of the First Lord, the First Sea Lord, the Permanent Secretary and three naval officers not members of the Board.

This development, a distinct step towards the divorce of executive from administrative duties, was, however, a source of internal weakness, for though it freed the other Sea Lords from operational work, it did not divest them of their joint responsibilities for actions over which they exercised no control. The Dardanelles operations was a case in point. They had never been consulted on the subject and yet, constitutionally, their responsibility for the undertaking was equal to that of the First Sea Lord, the only one of their number who had any voice in the matter. In 1914 the First Sea Lord was the only member of the Board who, according to instructions, was responsible for:

1. Preparation for war ; advice on all questions of naval policy and maritime warfare.

2. Fighting and seagoing efficiency of the Fleet, its organization and mobilization, etc.

3. Superintendence of the War Staff and hydrographic department.

It is obvious that under modern conditions these onerous and far-reaching duties are in war-time beyond the physical powers of any one man, for the conditions of naval warfare differ materially from those of military warfare. There is but one field of naval operations : the sea, extending to all parts of the globe, and naval forces are mobile to such a degree that every part of this vast field is a possible scene of action. For this geographical reason alone no naval Commander-in-Chief, however important the unit under his command, can be given that same strategic direction of naval forces that the Commander-in-Chief of land forces possesses in a well-defined area. But there are other physical reasons which render it impossible for a naval Commander to exercise a wide scope of authority. He with his Staff goes into action at the head of his forces and his flagship runs precisely the same risk of destruction as does any other unit of his Fleet; however, the size of his Staff is limited not by the amount of work to be done but by the space for their accommodation. Hence the Board of Admiralty in London must ever be the centre from which are conducted naval operations ; not from any undue centralization of power, but on account of fundamental differences between naval and military war conditions which are immutable.

When Mr. Churchill assumed the office of First

Lord in 1911 he sought to remedy this weakness by the creation of a War Staff which had never existed since the reconstruction of 1832. But he was handicapped in its development by the fact that there were at this time no naval officers of high rank who had had any experience of Staff work, hardly indeed of its need. The growth of the modern Navy had been rapid and the officers holding the higher ranks in the service during the first decade of the century had received their training in times when communications were slow and limited. Ships in those days were self-contained units whose intercourse with the outer world and with one another was leisurely and infrequent; the need for extended co-operation was consequently unfelt. But with the advent of wireless telegraphy this had all been changed. Head-quarters, were it Whitehall or a flagship, now received reports and information from all directions in such numbers and with such rapidity as to necessitate a large increase of personnel. Under the new conditions no one man was capable of keeping abreast of changing situations. Rapidity of decision became impossible unless authority were decentralized. But Admirals brought up to rely upon themselves and themselves alone, were distrustful of delegating their authority to others, and the newly formed War Staff remained a mere department devoid of any authority or responsibility until three years' experience of war proved the absolute necessity of its reconstruction on new lines.

Amongst those to whom the idea of an authoritative Staff could not be otherwise than repugnant must certainly be counted Lord Fisher, whose

18

mentality, in spite of his progressive views, was essentially of the old school. Delegation of authority must have appeared to him as a breach of discipline, perhaps even of trust. By far the most conspicuous naval figure of his time, he had filled with distinction every post of importance that it is possible for a naval officer to hold, and in each case had left a deep mark by the introduction of salutary reforms of a far-reaching nature. But he had carried them through by a ruthless bearing down of all opposition, without any attempt to disarm the natural dislike of an essentially conservative service, to whom the methods by which he sought to compass his ends were even more distasteful than the reforms themselves. Deprived therefore of the whole-hearted support of the greater part of the Navy, he had surrounded himself by a circle of clever and able naval officers, many of whom shared his opinions, though some were content to subordinate their views to his, whilst all of them hailed him as a genius. It has been claimed for him that he was the founder and the builder of the new Navy, and so far as its material side is concerned it is a just and true claim. In materiel, in discipline and in organization, the Fleet was, on the outbreak of war, in the highest state of efficiency, but at the Admiralty—where Lord Fisher as First Sea Lord had reigned supreme from 1906 to 1910, there was no indication of his reforming hand in the department charged with the conduct of war. The select ring had done nothing towards improving the organization by which war was to be conducted, though they had largely helped in perfecting the instrument by whose means it was to be waged.

The Navy was a splendid organism, ready for war and complete in every detail except one—and that one the most essential: a Staff necessary for its direction. Lord Fisher, with all his great qualities, his intellect and powers, was yet devoid of any comprehension of that greatest of modern requirements, organized co-operation—the welding together into an harmonious whole of the humblest as well as the greatest effort, i.e. what is commonly called team work.

Lord Fisher's return to the Admiralty, at Mr. Churchill's instance, in October 1914, caused much adverse criticism in naval circles. His second term of office lasted only seven months, but though short, was of sufficient duration to enable him to put in' hand with all his old vigour and enthusiasm an extensive new shipbuilding programme. Cruisers having many new features, monitors, destroyers and small craft were laid down in large numbers and eventually completed with a rapidity due to his initiative. He was instrumental in the destruction of Von Spee's Squadron off the Falkland Islands, but when he found himself faced with the Dardanelles problem, he failed. He was now in his seventy-fourth year, and whether increasing age, that seemingly had not diminished his energy, was sapping his powers or whether the fact that his appointment was chiefly due to political influence had deprived him of the independence necessary to withstand political pressure—whatever the true reason may have been—he failed. When he allowed himself to be dissuaded from resigning in January, he inevitably attached to himself some of the blame for the failure of the Dardanelles Campaign, and his resignation in May

was too late. The War Council was then too deeply
committed in the undertaking to permit of its
abandonment, and his resignation had no effect on
the course of naval events though it brought about
a political crisis.

Failure is seldom due to one cause only, and an
initial mistake invariably leads to others. So it
was in the Dardanelles Campaign. From the original
error of attacking the forts with ships alone, without awaiting the presence of an army to seize the
Gallipoli Peninsula, were derived that succession of
blunders leading to ultimate disaster that finally
came to an end on January 8, 1916. It is easy
to comprehend that the glamour of its potentialities
should have led the War Council, ignorant as they
were of its chances of success, to undertake the
operation, but difficult to understand how they
could have allowed themselves to be rushed into so
hazardous an enterprise without an exhaustive
study of the feasibility of carrying it out.

No one reading the report of the Dardanelles
Commission can fail to be struck by the fact that
not one of the Members of the War Council realized
that the first desideratum was possession of the
Gallipoli Peninsula, and that without it in our hands
even a successful issue of the naval attack would
have been abortive. And yet Sir Henry Jackson
had pointed out this essential fact to Mr. Churchill.
But the First Lord, eager to put in motion a project
that he believed would be attended by such por-
tentous results, was determined that nothing should
be allowed to stand in the way of its prosecution.
Even Lord Fisher's objections were insufficient to
cause him to hesitate in the course he was bent on

pursuing against professional advice, and he was able to convince his colleagues that a simultaneous naval and military attack was not essential to success.

Admiral Carden's plans had been submitted in reply to an inquiry as to whether he considered the forcing of the Dardanelles by the use of ships alone a practical operation. They had been drawn up without consideration of the possibility of maintaining communications after the work had been accomplished, or of the necessity of holding the Peninsula—two matters which were beyond the scope of his instructions. He had, as it turns out, under-estimated the power of mobile batteries to impede the operation. Though Sir Henry Jackson concurred in these plans, he had qualified his concurrence by recommending that only the first part of them, i.e., the destruction of the outer forts, should be undertaken. But Sir Henry Jackson had neither responsibility nor authority; he could only give advice; that done, his duty came to an end, and if the advice were not accepted there was nothing further he could do. And here we come to the flaw in the system;—the civilian Minister could legitimately press his plans on to the Council in spite of and in contradiction to professional advice.

It is clear that the committal of the first error was due to the faulty composition of the War Council, responsible for the inception of operations as a means towards attaining political ends. Strategy may perhaps be mastered without professional training, but a knowledge of tactics cannot be gained otherwise than technically, and it was owing to their ignoring professional advice on the tactical side of the question that the Council plunged into disaster.

Subsequent mistakes—lack of preparation, chaotic embarkation of the military expedition, shortage of ammunition and of drafts, delays in reinforcements, want of perception of the need of more extended naval co-operation—all derived their being from the original false step of which they were but the logical sequence, and when, at the end of August, it was evident that total failure could only be averted by a greater expenditure of force than was available, the hesitancy of the Government in deciding on what steps to adopt was the outcome of the false premise that the attack could be abandoned at will without loss of prestige and detrimental consequences.

That idea, as we know, began to fade away almost as soon as it had been born, and eventually, in the face of realities, disappeared altogether until after the failure of the August operations, when once more it took shape, not in its old form of voluntary withdrawal but in the new and unpleasant aspect of a forced retreat.

It was at this crisis that thoughts of further naval action began to materialize, for by this means only did chances offer of bringing the campaign to a successful end. But unsupported naval action was no more able to secure success now than at the beginning; combined action on the part of the land and sea forces was still a necessity. Would then a successful "rush" through the Straits so improve the position of our Army on the Peninsula as to make it possible for them to overcome the resistance of the enemy? Though no one could deny that the situation must thereby be changed, and not for the worse, the question could only be answered by military authorities, and therein lay the difficulty. No naval officer could answer that question, and yet without the Navy our position was untenable and the matter therefore not purely a military one. We on the spot were cut off from the naval and military authorities at home, where the decision lay, and thus debarred from hearing full arguments on both sides. Rightly or wrong-fully we believed that Sir Charles Monro had been sent out from England with a biassed opinion, and therefore was not in a position to form an objective judgment on the possible consequence of such action. I feared that whatever the decision it would not be the result of a co-ordinated review of the situation, and that those who in March had been so ready to precipitate us into the struggle without giving due weight to professional advice, would be equally hasty in retiring at all hazards.

There are those who believe that rushing the Straits was an unfeasible proposition that could only have resulted in disaster or in losses so heavy as to render nugatory the offensive powers of the survivors.

I did not think so then and after a lapse of eight years I see no reason to alter my opinion, either of the possibility of getting a squadron through the Straits or of the effect thereby produced. On the contrary, further experience has only confirmed the conviction that boldness and surprise, when allied to careful preparation and provision for all eventualities, are seldom lacking in success ; and though at Zeebrugge the conditions were not entirely simi-lar, there was sufficient analogy to justify the belief that the one assault would have been as triumphant as the other. Europe is at present in a state of chaos, due above all to the exhaustion caused by the long duration of the war which the occupation of Constantinople must inevitably have greatly shortened; any risks that the operation entailed seem therefore now even more justifiable than they did at the time.

Success would have reopened Russia's communications and saved her from Bolshevism and all its appalling consequences; failure was the direct cause of the prolonged and costly operations in Egypt, the tragic campaign in Mesopotamia. It lowered British prestige in the East, thus loosening our hold both on Egypt and India; indirectly it led to the disastrous Greco-Turkish policy and to the humiliating Treaty of Lausanne.

Politically and strategically the conception of the campaign was correct, and had it been properly planned and methodically carried out there is no reason why it should not have been crowned with success; but, rushed into as it was, without forethought or preparation, devoid of plan, treated as a side-issue, with improvisation as the only means whereby daily requirements could be met, it was little less than a crime, which could hardly have been committed had the body of men who sanctioned its inauguration been properly organized with a view to carrying out the work committed to their charge.

The losses incurred during this abortive campaign reached the stupendous figure of 120,246 and might well have been far greater had it not been for the good fortune in the matter of fine weather attending the evacuations, the possible casualties of which had been estimated at 30,000.

The blame for this tragedy cannot be laid at the door of any one individual, but must be attributed to system, the system that places the direction of naval and military operations solely in the hands of men devoid of the knowledge and experience necessary for the task, and immune, moreover, from the consequences of their actions; for the exercise of authority with the assurance of never being brought to account must ever be fraught with fatal results; and it is a noteworthy fact that not one of the members of the War Council responsible for the campaign but has held high office since its disastrous termination.

If wars are to be waged in the future, their direction should be confided to a body in which the political, naval and military elements should have their due proportion of authority and responsibility and whose duties are well defined. The creation of such a body should offer no difficulties, for its nucleus already exists in the Council of Imperial Defence which, with some readjustment, could readily be formed into the instrument sought. In its advisory capacity it performed invaluable services in peace; by investing it with executive power in war, it would render greater services still.

The existence of a competent Directive Council, prepared in peace time, even as are the Army and Navy, for the fulfilment of its duties in war, would go far towards preventing a repetition of like calamities, and in safe-guarding the interests of the nation and the lives of our soldiers and sailors.

As it is, mismanaged from the outset, starved of

the men and munitions which alone could ensure certain success, the cause of suffering greater than can be said, borne with a fortitude even greater, abandoned at the moment when victory was still within grasp, the campaign of the Dardanelles will remain through all ages to come an imperishable monument to the heroism of our race, to the courage and endurance of our soldiers and sailors, to the lack of vision and incapacity of our politicians.

FINIS

INDEX

Printed in Great Britain by Butler & Tanner Ltd., Frome and London

Lightning Source UK Ltd.
Milton Keynes UK
UKOW03f0356021014

239477UK00001B/221/P